GERARD CHALIAND

THE
KURDISH TRAGEDY

Translated by Philip Black

ZED BOOKS LTD
London & New Jersey

in association with
UNRISD

THE KURDISH TRAGEDY
was first published in English in 1994
by Zed Books Ltd
7 Cynthia Street, London N1 9JF
and 165 First Avenue, Atlantic Highlands,
New Jersey 07716, USA
in association with the
United Nations Research Institute for
Social Development (UNRISD),
Palais des Nations 1211, Geneva 10, Switzerland

French edition commissioned by UNRISD
and published in 1992 by Editions du Seuil
under the title *Le malheur kurde*

Copyright © Editions du Seuil 1992
Translation copyright © Philip Black 1994

Cover design by Andrew Corbett
Cover photo copyright © F Horval/Saba–Select
Maps courtesy Catherine Petit and Martin Van Bruinessen
Printed and bound in the UK
by Biddles Ltd, Guildford and King's Lynn

A catalogue record for this book
is available from the British Library
US CIP is available from the Library of Congress

ISBN 1 85649 099 8 Hb
1 85649 100 5 Pb

Table of Contents

The United Nations Research Institute for Social Development (UNRISD) is an autonomous research organisation focusing on the most pressing social problems of development. Its work is inspired by the conviction that, for effective development to be formulated, an understanding of the social and political context is crucial, as is an accurate assessment of how such policies affect different social groups. While multidisciplinary research programmes are designed by a small staff in Geneva and external co-ordinators, they are carried out in collaboration with national research teams drawn from local universities and research institutes, mainly in developing countries

Current research programmes include: Sustainable Development through People's Participation in Resource Management; Social Dynamics of Deforestation in Developing Countries; Impact of Agricultural Expansion on the Sustainable Management of Tropical Forests; Women, Environment and Population; Population Dynamics, Environmental Change and Development Processes; Crisis, Adjustment and Social Change; Participation and Changes in Property Relations in Communist and Post-Communist Societies; Ethnic Conflict and Development; Political Violence and Social Movements; Refugees, Returnees and Local Society; Socio-Economic and Political Impact of Production, Trade and Use of Illicit Narcotic Drugs; and Qualitative Indicators of Development

A list of publications can be obtained by writing: Reference Centre, UNRISD, Palais des Nations, CH-1211 Geneva, Switzerland.

Regions populated by the Kurds

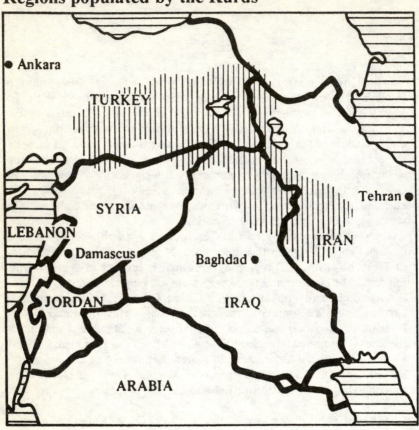

Regions inhabited by the Kurdish Nation

Dialects spoken in Kurdistan

|||||||| northern Kurdish dialects   \\\\\\\ southern Kurdish dialects

///// Zaza dialects   ———— southeastern Kurdish dialects

🌢. Gurani dialects

Iraqi Kurdistan

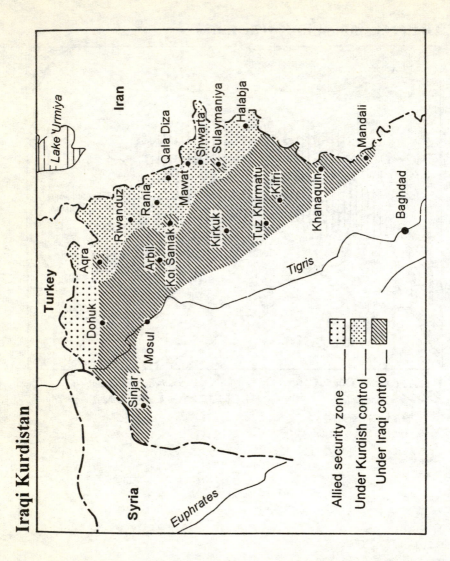

Allied security zone —
Under Kurdish control —
Under Iraqi control —

Preface

The Kurdish question

During the final days of March 1991, in an immense exodus broadcast live by the television networks of the West, some 1.5 million Kurds were propelled towards Iran and the approaches of the Turkish border. This exodus, the result of the terror inspired by the elite troops of Saddam Hussein's regime, brought to an end the spontaneous insurrection that had given the Kurds ephemeral control over Iraqi Kurdistan.

Following the Gulf War, the *Shi'ites*, who make up just over half the population of Iraq, concentrated mainly in the south of the country, rebelled and took control of the main southern towns. Saddam Hussein's regime reacted swiftly and brutally. The danger of the *Shi'ites* taking over Iraq, or exercising an influence proportional to their share of the population, was averted.

This is precisely why Saddam Hussein, with the help of Saudi Arabian pressure on the United States, remained in power, and why the ground war came to an end, with the National Guard, the strong arm of the regime, still operational. The survival of the *Sunni* minority at the head of the country was ensured. This strategic minority — some 22 per cent of the population — has been in power since the British created Iraq after the end of the First World War. It remains important for Saudi Arabia that there should be no strengthening of a *Shi'ite* community, having more in common with Iran than with the Wahhabi monarchy, so close to its vulnerable borders.

On 6th March a spontaneous uprising broke out in the important Kurdish village of Ranya, a few dozen kilometres from the Iranian border. Ever since June 1990, Ranya, like many other Kurdish villages, had been living under the threat of being wiped off the map and its population moved to a more controllable area. On the same day, the Kurds took over the police stations and barracks, arrested the local Ba'ath representatives and generally took the situation under control. The insurrection was fast and completely successful, incurring hardly any losses. It spread like wild-fire.

In the eight days from 6th to 14th March, the main urban centres of Arbil and Sulaymaniya fell, one after the other, under the weight of popular pressure. The Kurdish political movements were taken by surprise and could do nothing but join in with this wave of passionate feelings that they had neither engineered nor foreseen. After some fighting, Dohuk fell. As of the 14th March the *peshmergas* of the Unified Kurdistan Front decided to take control of Kirkuk, the country's second town, whose status had for a long time been a bone of contention between Baghdad and the Kurds.

After four days of fighting, a large part of the military base fell to the insurgents. Iraq decided to send in its air force and on 22nd March an Iraqi SU 22 was shot down by the allies. However, the United States let it be known that they would not object to the use of helicopters to put down the uprising, which now extended across the whole of Iraqi Kurdistan.

The ground-based counter-offensive of Baghdad's elite troops began on 27th March. As the *peshmergas* only had light arms, the towns were recaptured quickly and the repression was brutal, particularly in Dohuk. The population, overcome by panic and fearing massive repression as well as a repeat of the 1988 use of chemical weapons, fled *en masse* towards the borders. According to different sources, between 1.5 and 2 million people tried to escape from the advancing Iraqi troops. About two thirds crossed the Iranian border and approximately 600,000 people crowded into the approaches of the Turkish frontier.

The altitude and prevailing cold of the region during those last winter days made the situation even worse. The Kurds were experiencing the most tragic hours of their history since the great repressions and deportations of the 1920s and 1930s in Turkey. However, this time, the involvement of the United States, Great Britain and France in the Gulf War put the Kurds, at long last, at the centre of international current events.

On 2nd April, in the United Nations Security Council, the French called for humanitarian intervention. Great Britain quickly allied itself with the French position.

On the other hand, on 4th April, the president of the United States ruled out any intervention of a military nature which might put 'precious American lives' at risk. On 5th April, the Security Council of the UN condemned the repression of the civilian population and asked Baghdad to facilitate access for international humanitarian organisations. That same day, under pressure from France, Great Britain and Turkey, who did not want to see over half a million Kurdish refugees settling on her territory, the American president agreed to launch an operation to bring humanitarian aid to the refugees. The first supplies were parachuted in on 7th April.

On 8th April, the Twelve approved the British proposal to set up a 'safe haven' for the Kurds under United Nations mandate, but the proposal was rejected by the United States.

On the 10th, Washington banned Baghdad from conducting any airborne operation in the north of Iraq.

On the 16th, the president of the United States finally agreed to a ground-based intervention on Iraqi soil. From 20th April American soldiers, soon to be reinforced by British and French contingents, arrived in Zakho close to the Turkish border and established an allied 'security zone'.

In the meantime, a strong feeling of solidarity with the Kurdish people was becoming apparent, particularly in western Europe and North America.

Even Turkey authorised a nation-wide collection for humanitarian aid for the Kurds. During the whole period of the tragic Kurdish exodus, however, there was no reaction from any of the countries of the Arab world.

For the first time since 1920, the Kurdish question was being debated by official organisations, and, at France's request, by the United Nations Security Council which passed resolution 688, (see Appendix 1), recognising its obligation to intervene on humanitarian grounds.

On 24th April, after several days of negotiations in Baghdad, the Kurdish movements of the Unified Front, whose two most important representatives were Jalal Talabani of the Patriotic Union of Kurdistan (PUK) and Masoud Barzani of the Kurdistan Democratic Party of Iraq (KDP-Iraq), reached an 'agreement of principle on the status of Iraqi Kurdistan'. This dramatic turn of events was the indirect result of the presence of allied troops in the security zone in northern Iraq and on the Turkish border.

The agreement of principle on autonomy was based on an earlier agreement on the autonomy of Kurdistan, which Saddam Hussein had proposed in March 1970. One of the obstacles that the 1970 agreement had come up against was the status of the oil-rich town of Kirkuk. This setback led to the resumption of hostilities and the collapse in 1975 of the Kurdish movement whose leader at the time was Mustafa Barzani.

The halting progress of the negotiations during the summer was a very bad sign. As the Allied disengagement continued, the Kurdish movements failed to achieve their essential objective, an agreement on autonomy — even, if necessary, a more modest one than the one they were demanding — guaranteed by the international authorities. Failing this, they can be assured that, true to himself, Saddam Hussein will wait for the most favourable moment to regain control of the situation with his usual brutal determination.

The Kurds have the twofold distinction of having been, for the past sixty-five years, one of the most heavily repressed minorities and one of the most numerous, with a population of some 20 to 25 million individuals spread unevenly between Turkey, Iran and Iraq. There is also a small Kurdish settlement in Syria[1]. Present in the Ottoman Empire and Persia until the end of the First World War, the Kurds were soon divided into three and even four countries. Great Britain, after receiving the Mesopotamian mandate following the collapse of the Ottoman Empire, united the two Arab *vilayets* (provinces) of Baghdad and Basra with the *vilayet* of Mosul, whose oil reserves were known to the British and whose status was to remain uncertain until 1925. Mosul had a majority Kurdish population at the time.[2]

The treaty of Sèvres, which anticipated the creation of a Kurdish state in the south-east of today's Turkey, was rendered null and void by the energy and determination of Mustafa Kemal, admirably supported by a section of the empire's military commanders. This war of national independence, waged mainly against the Greeks, but also against the French mandate in Cilicia and the Armenian state (1918-1920), was widely supported by the Kurds in the name of Moslem solidarity.

A section of the Turkish elite had, on the other hand, adopted the European notion of modern nationalism.[3] After the signing of the treaty of Lausanne (1923) which guaranteed him full sovereignty, Mustafa Kemal, thirty years before Nasser, enthusiastically embraced a policy mix of narrowly nationalist zeal and modernisation (suppression of the caliphate, introduction of a system of common law, romanisation of the alphabet, etc.).

In 1924, the Kurdish language was banned. The Kurds thus lost, by decree, their very identity, since no one in Turkey could be anything but Turkish, unless they belonged to one of the landless religious minorities whose rights were recognised in the treaty of Lausanne. These consisted of some tens of thousands of Armenians who still remained in Turkey after the 1915-1916 deportation and massacre in transit of the entire Armenian population of Anatolia;[4] the Greeks, equally few in number after the physical elimination of those of the Pontus (1915-1916) and the massive population exchanges (1,250,000 Greeks against 650,000 Turks) following the Greek defeat; finally a small community of Sephardic Jews who had been welcomed and well treated when the Jews were expelled from Spain.

The treaty of Lausanne recognised no other minorities, nor did it grant this status to the Kurds, despite the fact that from 1918 to 1923 they had acted as loyal allies to their Turkish co-religionists.

Unlike the Armenians and the Arabs of Syria, the few modernist Kurdish elites of the period did not grasp that the defeat of the Ottoman Empire opened up entirely new possibilities.

Meanwhile, the Kemalists quickly filled the power vacuum left by the Sultan, thereby frustrating Greek, French and Armenian aspirations to take advantage of the situation.

A Kurdish delegation did attend the peace conferences in an attempt to gain acceptance of Kurdish demands. However, the absence of an enlightened intelligentsia along with the general backwardness of Kurdish society blocked the spread of any nationalist ideology imported from Europe. Despite the existence at the time of a few modernist influenced groups, it wasn't until the 1940s that Kurdish political organisations gradually began to take shape.

Even after that, Kurdish political organisations were marked by the tribal conflicts characteristic of a segmented society. There were many personal rivalries between their leaders, who were usually drawn from families of religious or tribal dignitaries. The conflicts between the Marxists and non-Marxists of the 1960s, 1970s and beyond, were often ancient tribal power struggles in a modern guise.

The great rebellions of the 19th century had been uprisings, at the heart of the Ottoman Empire, of traditional religious or non-religious leaders against the Sublime Porte's ever more strictly enforced policies of centralisation. The rebellions of the 1920s and 1930s in Turkey, Iraq and, to a lesser extent, in Iran, were expressions of a mixture of religious conservatism (in Turkey), regional insurrection (in all three countries) and local patriotism tinged with nationalist demands. There were no programmes, political organisations, or cadres. There was no overall co-ordination; no overcoming of family, tribal, or regional rivalries.

The Kurds were no match for the old states of Turkey and Iran, with their diplomatic, political and military traditions. In Iraq, where their numbers are proportionally greater,[5] the situation was better, in so far as it was not possible for the *Sunnis* in power to dominate the political scene with the same efficiency as the Turks or the Persians — at least not until the mid 1970s.

The geographical isolation of the Kurdish regions, with no access to the sea, makes it easy to understand the Kurdish political organisations' constant search for external alliances, particularly from the 1960s onwards. The USSR, the United States and Israel have all played the Kurdish card to weaken, indirectly, a regional adversary. At the beginning of the 1960s, Iran supported the Kurds of Iraq. However, nobody, either from fear of the internal repercussions or from fear of contagion, would consider helping the Kurds achieve a real political victory.

Moreover, from the 1960s onwards, the ambiguous situations created when a state was giving support to a Kurdish movement in a neighbouring and rival state, while at the same time repressing another one at home, provoked an outbreak of conflicts between the different Kurdish parties, as in the case of the relations between the Kurdish political organisations of Iraq and Iran during the 1960s and beyond.

During the war between Iraq and Iran (1980-1988), each of the two states gave military support to the Kurdish movement opposed to its rival. The Kurds of Iran were aided by Iraq; those of Iraq by Iran (and sometimes by Syria, Iraq's Ba'athist rival). It is nearly always easier for a state to win a complex game of this sort than it is for a movement that risks finding itself suddenly deprived of support.

Dominated by Turks, Persians and Arabs, the Kurds are confronted with policies that vary from one state to another. Turkey's approach to cultural assimilation is the most systematic. In this respect Iran operates a more open policy; even though Kurdish is not taught in the schools, at least the state broadcasts programmes in the Kurdish language.

On the other hand Iraq accepts Kurdish as its second official language and recognises the principle of autonomy, on condition that it remains completely under the control of the Ba'ath party.

Mass deportations or the resettlement of populations into areas where they could be more easily controlled were used by Turkey throughout the 1920s and 1930s and, given a decree issued in 1990, could be used again. These methods were also used by Iraq after 1975 and, in an increasingly systematic way, at the end of the 1980s. We do not yet know all the consequences of the mass exodus of March-April 1991 that propelled perhaps a million refugees towards Iran, not to mention all those who ended up in camps along the Turkish border.

There has been no major industrial investment in Kurdish areas by any of the three states. The poverty of their infrastructures is patent, the health and education systems widely deficient. In each of the three countries, there is considerable Kurdish emigration towards large towns situated outside Kurdish areas.[6]

It has been official policy in Turkey from 1924 until the last few years to deny the very existence of a Kurdish minority. The Turkish sociologist Ismail Besikçi has spent more than a decade in prison for having written about the existence of the Kurds and of Kurdish particularism. Nevertheless the Kurds are an ethnic minority with a language totally unrelated to the Turkish family of languages. Formerly known as the 'Mountain Turks', in recent years they have at last achieved open mention in the press. During the Gulf War, the Turkish president, Mr Ozal, even announced the lifting of the 1983 ban on speaking Kurdish in public.[7]

The Kurds of Turkey have been granted no other rights: neither the right to learn Kurdish at school; nor the right to publish officially in that language. Since 1990, the extraordinary powers available to the governor of those provinces in a state of emergency due to the guerilla activities of the Workers' Party of Kurdistan (PKK)[8] leave the population with virtually no rights.

The Turkish state, relying sometimes on traditional leaders, sometimes on elements of the urban population, had endeavoured to enforce, within the limits of its capabilities, a policy of 'turkisation'. This policy came up against, on the one hand the underdevelopment of the Kurdish regions, which were still far from having any universal school system in which Turkish was compulsorily taught, and, on the other hand, from the 1960s and particularly from the 1970s, the awakening of Kurdish particularism.

Nevertheless, in the large towns of western and central Anatolia, amongst Kurds urbanised for over a generation, whose children have been taught Turkish at school, this cultural integration seems to have succeeded. In these areas Kurdishness is being reduced to the status of folklore. Some Kurds — although never as such — have been or are parliamentary deputies, even ministers. The most famous success story is that of the novelist Yashar Kemal, a Kurd but a Turkish author who writes exclusively in Turkish and does not refer to his origins.

The opposite example is that of the Kurdish film director Yilmaz Güney[9] whose films are in Turkish, but who has laid great stress on his ethnic identity and has been an active campaigner for the recognition of Kurdish rights.

Until recently, the great fear of the Turkish authorities was that the use of the Kurdish language, and the political ends to which it might be put, would sooner or later break up the cohesion of the Jacobin national state defined by Mustafa Kemal. One could, of course, argue to the contrary, as do certain Turkish liberals, who insist that the root of the Kurdish problem in Turkey lies in the cultural negation that has been official policy since 1924.

The present situation in the Kurdish regions of Turkey, subjected to a state of emergency with particularly repressive laws, would hardly seem to favour any fundamental reforms. Since 1984, priority has been given to counter-insurgency measures against the PKK, with frequent incursions by the Turkish army across the Iraqi border.

However, the Turkish position is being modified, at least in so far as the official existence of the Kurds in Turkey is concerned. In February 1988, the Turkish government complained when a report of the US State Department mentioned a Kurdish minority on its territory and criticised Turkey for infringements of the human rights of this minority.[10]

The State Department's report described the situation in the following manner: 'Even though millions of Kurdish Turks are fully integrated into the political, economic and social life of the nation, the policy of complete assimilation conducted by the (Turkish) government has led to a ban on the publication of any book, newspaper or other material in the Kurdish language. Anything that deals with Kurdish history, culture or ethnic identity is proscribed and there have been cases of the arrest of performers for singing or acting in Kurdish. The preceding limits on cultural expression are a genuine source of discontent amongst many Turks of Kurdish origin, particularly in the economically less developed south-east where they are in the majority.'[11]

In recent years the press has begun to question Kemalist dogmas. In April 1991 Mr Ozal told the Turkish newspaper *Tercuman* that it might be possible to find a solution to the Kurdish problem 'based on the Basque model'. If he was referring to the autonomy given to the Basques and other groups by Spain, then there remains a long way to go since, for the time being, only the ban on speaking Kurdish in public has been lifted.

In Iraq, the opposition between the Kurds and the Iraqi government has followed a specific pattern for the past three decades. Any administration in a position of weakness in Baghdad engages in negotiations with the Kurdish movement, which demands autonomy within the framework of Iraq. These negotiations drag on long enough for Baghdad to rebuild its offensive potential. In the best of cases, an agreement is signed, like the one of 11th March 1970 recognising an autonomous status for Kurdistan. Then the negotiations come to a standstill over the definition of the territorial basis of Kurdistan, over the areas rich in oil reserves, over the distribution of revenues, etc. A fresh confrontation erupts whenever the government feels it has the means to emerge as the winner. From then on, a renewed weakening of authority is necessary, either through a change of regime or a war, before the Kurds can again exert pressure on Baghdad.

From all the evidence, the present negotiations between Saddam Hussein and the Kurdish leaders of Iraq are conforming to the same rules. The Iraqi head of state is trying to gain time, while the Kurds attempt to extract on paper an agreement that will be violated tomorrow.

In Iran, integration into Persian culture is open to both Kurds and Azeris. However, neither the Kurds nor the Azeris have ever had the right to study their own language at school.

The situation today is not hopeful. From 1925 to 1930, Reza Shah's policy was that of a brutal bringing to heel of the semi-nomadic tribes that had always sought to escape from central state control. The uprising led by the Kurdish chief, Simko, was progressively ground down and its leader assassinated during the course of peace negotiations. Following the founding of a republic at Mahabad immediately after the end of the Second World War, events moved fast. The situation that had led to the establishment of this short-lived republic, crushed a year later by the Iranian army, stemmed from two factors: that in 1945 the state of Iran no longer controlled the north of the country and that the Soviet Union was determined to extend its influence by supporting the creation both of an Azerbaijani republic and of a (Kurdish) republic of Mahabad in Iran. The latter, with its uncertain status, equipped itself with all the attributes of autonomy, along with a military force, and developed completely independently of Tehran. Once the British re-established themselves in Iran, the Shah was given the means to regain control. All the leaders of the Mahabad republic were hung. Mustafa Barzani, who had been in charge of the armed forces, managed to beat a path to the Soviet Union, where he found refuge and remained until the downfall of the Hashemite monarchy in Iraq (1958).

From 1946, the Kurdistan Democratic Party of Iran (KDPI) was outlawed and its activists hunted down, tortured and imprisoned. The KDPI, at the time close to the Tudeh, the Iranian Communist Party, supported Mossadegh's nationalist and 'anti-imperialist' experiment until he was overthrown in 1953 with the active collusion of the CIA. Once again, the KDPI endured a severe repression. In the 1960s there was a rural uprising in the Kurdish regions. It was crushed. Relations between the Iraqi KDP and the Iranian KDP became strained. Indeed, Mustafa Barzani, who had taken control of an important armed faction struggling for autonomy in Iraq, and was receiving aid from Iran, handed over to the Iranian authorities, at their request, a number of cadres of the KDPI who had taken refuge in Iraq.

It wasn't until the demonstrations against the Shah in 1978 that the KDPI, under the leadership of Abdul Rahman Ghassemlou, was once again to play an active role. The KDPI took part in the demonstrations in the towns, notably at Mahabad, which resulted in the rout and collapse of the regime.

In 1979 a *de facto* autonomy was established in Iranian Kurdistan. But the Ayatollah's regime, like the subsequent one of the *mullahs*, drew the line at autonomy. During the war between Iraq and Iran, the *pasdaran* (revolutionary guards) conducted several campaigns to regain control of Iranian Kurdistan. As the years went by, the Kurdish forces mustered on the other side of the border, in Iraq.

The official negotiations which A.R. Ghassemlou entered into with envoys from the Iranian government in July 1989 ended with his assassination in Vienna by the Iranian delegates, just as Simko had been murdered thirty years earlier.

In Syria, where the Kurds do not occupy a continuous stretch of territory, they have not been granted any cultural rights. The situation for the Kurds was particularly difficult during the 1960s, when population transfers were carried out to facilitate the resettlement of the Arab populations. With the coming to power of Hafiz al-Asad and the Alawites — who only make up some 15 per cent of the total population — the situation changed, although there has been no improvement as far as rights are concerned. Since the Alawites are very much in the minority themselves, they need the support of other minorities. As long as they collaborate, material circumstances for some Kurds are much better than before Asad came to power. This ambiguous situation could deteriorate swiftly were the present regime to fall.

The contemporary history of the Kurds can be divided into several important stages:

Stage 1: 1920-1945

During this period, when the Kurds were split between three, and even four countries, the sovereign states of the Middle East — Turkey, Iran and soon Iraq — applied, without hindrance, alternating policies of assimilation and repression, while confining a large part of the Kurdish population to regions with limited resources. Where these resources existed — for example the oil deposits of Kirkuk — no profits ever found their way back to the Kurdish people.

This was the stage when the great uprisings in Turkey (1925, 1930, 1936-1937) were crushed with extreme brutality, followed by deportations.

Foreigners were banned from the Kurdish regions until 1965, whilst officially the Kurds of Turkey simply did not exist. This negation of reality is almost unique in the 20th century, akin to Turkey's continuing denial of its 1915 genocide against the Armenians.

In Iraq, while the status of the *vilayet* of Mosul remained undecided until 1925, a succession of rebellions took place between 1920 and 1943, led by Shaikh Mahmud,[12] then by the Barzanis.

Stage 2: 1945-1958

The setting up of the republic of Mahabad (1945), despite its short-lived existence, lasting for barely a year, was a milestone. Even though traditional leaders and dignitaries continued to play a dominant role, this period saw the emergence of parties, the beginnings of an administrative organisation and the first experience of the management of a political system along modern lines.

Afterwards, repression and silence prevailed in Turkey, Iran and Iraq until 1958.

Stage 3: 1958-1975

This stage was the consequence of General Qasim's *coup d'état*, which brought to an end the Hashemite dynasty in Iraq. His recognition of Iraq as the homeland of two peoples, Arab and Kurd, was something entirely new.

When the Kurdish question re-emerged in Iraq, after a dozen years of total silence, the world had changed a great deal. The colonial and semi-colonial era was virtually moribund. Asia had become independent. In North Africa, only Algeria was not yet independent, but its war of liberation had international support. Ghana had acquired its independence. In the period between the proclamation of the Iraqi republic (1958) and Mustafa Barzani's taking up of arms (1961) in an attempt to impose the autonomy of Kurdistan within the context of Iraq, the greater part of Africa achieved independence. However, the only peoples who achieved their right to self-determination were those once colonised by Europeans.[13] The Kurds did not fall into this category. They were the citizens of states with a despotic tradition, where it was considered dangerous and unnecessary to grant rights to a minority.

This was the period when the Kurdish movement of Iraq revived, this time in the context of the Cold War. With the Truman doctrine only just defined, the USSR was already being countered and blocked, not only in Greece (during the civil war) and in Turkey (Soviet claims on Kars and Ardahan), but also in Iran with the elimination of the republics of Azerbaijan and Mahabad. At the time, the Kurds of Iraq and Iran were considered to be pro-Soviet and indeed the USSR had many friends and supporters amongst them.

From 1961 to 1975, the Kurds of Iraq experienced the bitterness of political alliances. Barzani's movement was dropped by the Soviet Union which preferred an alliance with the state of Iraq, signing a treaty of friendship and co-operation with Saddam Hussein's regime in 1972. Following a decision by Nixon and Kissinger, clandestine aid from the National Security Council came to replace Soviet assistance: the alliance between Iraq and the USSR worried the United States. The state of Israel also was more than willing to provide clandestine assistance aimed at weakening an Arab state that was a member of the Rejection Front. The Iranians, of whom Barzani was always unsure, in contrast to the confidence he had in the United States, withdrew their support in 1975, realising that it was no longer in their interest to support the Iraqi Kurds, given the concessions granted to them by Iraq. For the Kurds, this second half of the 1970s was a grim period of failure and stagnation.

Stage 4: 1975-1993

The fall of the Shah (1978) and the war between Iraq and Iran (1980) allowed the Iranian KDP to resurface and, for a relatively brief period, to create the conditions of a *de facto* autonomy. The two states then each made use of the other's Kurds to contribute to a weakening of their rival.

The Iraqi movements, sometimes aided by Iran, sometimes by Syria, grew in strength sufficiently to arouse Turkish anxieties about the sanctuary that the PKK had found in Iraq since 1983. Indeed the resurgence of Kurdish movements, in Turkey as elsewhere, was one of the salient features of the 1970s. The PKK was the toughest of these movements, and the only one to switch to armed struggle. The existence of PKK bases in Iraq led to a number of raids by the Turkish army into Iraq since 1983.

As soon as the Iran-Iraq war was over, Saddam Hussein's regime sought to subdue the Kurdish militants by depriving them of all popular support. 1988 was marked by a series of offensives, with the use of chemical weapons as well as massive bombardments. The martyrdom of the little town of Halabja became known through pictures on western television stations, even though Iraq denied using gas, and Turkey — having sheltered some of the refugees — announced that it could find no trace of chemical weapons, while at the same time refusing an international inspection.

In 1988 and at the beginning of 1989, Saddam Hussein's regime continued to pursue its ten-year-old policy: the systematic relocation of Kurdish populations into lowland areas after the destruction of their mountain villages. The figures cited vary: according to official American sources, out of a total of just over 5,000 villages, 1,200 were destroyed and resettled. Kurdish sources put the figure at 3,500.

In any case, the events of March-April 1991 greatly accentuated the effects of this long-term policy, by creating the greatest Kurdish exodus in history, and the most important global exodus since that of the people of Afghanistan towards Pakistan in 1980, which took place far less abruptly, and over an extended period.

So how does the balance sheet stand today at the end of several decades of demands pursued by both violent and non-violent means? Following the assassination of A.R. Ghassemlou the situation in Iran is stagnant: the state has established military control over Iranian Kurdistan. In Iraq, the negotiations between Baghdad and the unified Kurdistan Front provided Saddam Hussein with a breathing space, allowing him to wait until the allies had stopped protecting the 'security zone' where the Kurds enjoy a *de facto* autonomy. For the Kurdish movements, the stalemate is a result of the political inability of their leadership to extract an international guarantee concerning the status of autonomy. According to the United Nations High Commission for Refugees, the Iraqi army's bombardments in November-December 1991 caused a further 200,000 Kurdish refugees to be added to the 500,000 already recorded.

In Turkey, where the press has been discussing the Kurds for a number of years, Mr Ozal's first positive initiative was to repeal the 1983 law prohibiting the speaking of Kurdish in public. In addition, during the Gulf War, perhaps for reasons that seemed to him opportune at the time, the Turkish president mentioned the existence of 12 million Kurds in Turkey (that is to say 20 per cent of the total population). On 8th December 1991, the new Turkish Prime Minister Mr Demirel confirmed Mr Ozal's initiative by recognising the 'Kurdish reality'. Nevertheless no further initiative has yet been taken concerning any eventual cultural rights.

After thirty years which have cost the Kurds so dear — not to mention what they suffered during the 1920s and 1930s — the balance sheet does appear to be somewhat deficient.

Given the geopolitical realities, can the Kurds, whether it be in Turkey, in Iran or in Iraq, hope to achieve by force of arms the autonomy they are calling for in Iran and in Iraq, or the independence that the PKK maintains it can achieve in Turkey? This seems to be out of the question.

In a world where the Cold War has just ended, and with it the need to pander to the sensibilities of this or that ally, it is surely time for the democratic countries within the United Nations to push for a change in the rules of the international game. The United Nations' failure in 1962 to prevent Ethiopia from incorporating within its empire autonomous Eritrea — which had been the UN's own creation — became the source of a conflict that lasted thirty years. It is unquestionably time that the United Nations became committed, in a certain number of cases, to making sure that agreements between a state and a minority are respected.

It is becoming increasingly necessary for the UN to address the rights of minorities, whenever there is a flagrant violation of the minimum standards recognised by international laws. Of all the minorities that have suffered oppression over the last sixty-five years, the Kurds have undoubtedly been amongst those who have paid the highest price.

Notes

1. We shall not deal here with the small Kurdish community of the former USSR, who have no territory of their own, being dispersed over at least three or four republics, and whose study fits into a quite different context.

2. In 1923, the population of the *vilayet* of Mosul was made up as follows: 58 per cent Kurds, 23 per cent Arabs, 19 per cent others.

3. It is difficult to imagine just how alien the ideology of modern nationalism was to the Middle East, right up to the First World War, except amongst sections of a very narrow urban elite.

4. These events have been recognised as 'genocide' by the UN Council on Human Rights (1986) and by the Council of Europe (1987). Turkey, however, still opposes this characterisation.

5. The Kurds account for roughly 25 per cent of the population in Iraq, 20 per cent in Turkey and 15 per cent in Iran.

6. It is also worth noting the presence of half a million Kurdish workers in western Europe, including 400,000 in Germany and 60,000 in France.

7. The 1983 legislation stipulated that 'The mother tongue of Turkish citizens is Turkish'.

8. Elazig, Bingöl, Tunceli, Van, Diyarbekir, Mardin, Sirt, Hakkeri, Batman and Sirnak.

9. Yilmaz Güney won the *Grand Prix du festival de Cannes* in 1982 for his film *Yol*. All Yilmaz Güney's films are banned in Turkey.

10. Michael M. Gunter, *The Kurds of Turkey: A Political Dilemma*, Westport, Greenwood Press, 1991, p.117.

11. *Country Reports on Human Rights Practices for 1988*, US Congress Senate Committee on Foreign Affairs, 101st congress, 1st session, 1989, p.7 (cited in M.Gunter, *op. cit*, p.123).

12. With the exception of the 1930 insurrection in Turkey and that led by Simko in Iran, from 1925 — 1930, all the revolts were led by religious leaders.

13. With the sole exception of Eritrea, an ex-Italian colony entrusted to Ethiopia as an autonomous territory by the United Nations in 1952. Ten years later, the Emperor of Ethiopia proclaimed Eritrea as the fourteenth province of his empire. Thus began a conflict which has only recently come to an end, with the fall of Mengistu and the new regime's agreement to allow a referendum on self-determination in Eritrea before 1993.

1. The Kurdish Identity

The geographical term 'Kurdistan', which has never signified a state, was used under the Ottoman Empire to denote a territory equivalent to the province of Diyarbakir in the Turkey of today. Similarly in Iran, the province called Kurdistan is only one of the regions which is ethnically Kurdish.

As a majority population, the Kurds occupy a strategic crossroads situated mainly between Turkey, Iran and Iraq. Frequently referred to by the geographical term 'Kurdistan', this country of high mountains was often used as a place of refuge during successive waves of invasions over the centuries. The Taurus mountains (in modern Turkey) and the Zagros (in Iran), are mountain chains facing north-west/south-east whose heights overlook the Mesopotamian plain. Towards the north and north-east are high plateaux where the Armenian populations were based before they were progressively driven out by the Kurds over the last two centuries. The genocide of the Armenians in 1915 turned the Armenian plateau into a mainly Kurdish population zone. The territorial area of Kurdish population, in relation to that of the Arabs in the south and that of the Azeris in the east, is clearly demarcated: the Kurds occupy the mountain areas. But in the north-west the Kurdish and Turkish populations are intermixed, sometimes closely.

Geographical Kurdistan is very continental and winters there are particularly harsh. Travellers tales tell us that Kurdistan was still very wooded a century ago. Deforestation caused by demographic pressure and the need for firewood is today a serious problem for agriculture, having caused accelerated soil erosion.

Geographical Kurdistan harbours reserves of chromium, copper, iron, coal and lignite, but its main wealth is oil. There are oil fields at Mosul, Kirkuk and Khanaqin in Iraq.

Since none of the countries concerned has made a census of its Kurds, only approximations of Kurdish demography can be established, varying considerably from one author to another. It is estimated that some 12 million Kurds live in Turkey, around 4 million in Iraq, over 7 million in Iran and a community of about a million in Syria. In total there are probably some 25 million Kurds, split up unevenly between these four countries.

Contrary to popular belief, only a small fraction of the Kurdish population is nomadic. Most are farmers and, to a much lesser extent, stockbreeders. The mountains afford no more than a subsistence level economy, whereas the plains of Syria and Iraq provide good yields of grain. Tobacco is a traditional crop in Iran, Iraq and south-eastern Turkey whilst the introduction of cotton in Turkey is recent. As a general rule, in the mountain areas where traditional methods of farming are still used, the peasants own their land, whereas in the plains large landowners depend on tenant farmers and, increasingly, on agricultural workers. The latter being able to find work only on a seasonal basis, a pattern of migrations evolved from the 1950s onwards. The living conditions of smallholders have gradually deteriorated as demographic pressure led to the break up of landholdings.

Economic migration towards the industrial towns during the past few decades has partly drained the Kurdish regions, particularly in Turkey, of their productive population. Political difficulties and the state policy-derived inadequacy of the infrastructures discourage investment in the Kurdish regions where, with the exception of oil extraction, industry is almost non-existent. Tobacco production could be increased, but the state monopolies in Iran, Iraq and Turkey have slowed down development.

Specialised craft work in Kurdistan was for a long time a monopoly of the Christian and Jewish minorities. The towns of Diyarbakir, Bitlis, Van, Arbil and Mosul were centres of commerce and production where the non-Kurdish element predominated, while the countryside remained relatively self-sufficient in the production of everyday objects until the beginning of the century.

The rapid decline of craft work in Kurdistan is first of all linked to the disappearance of the religious minorities. The Armenians were deported and massacred during the First World War, and, more generally, the Christian communities were at that time expelled from Anatolia. The creation of the state of Israel was later to bring with it the emigration of almost all oriental Jewish communities. The craft of wool production, which was an Armenian speciality, has greatly declined; similarly the irrigation systems of the Christian villages, more advanced than those of the Kurds, have not been maintained.

The other factor which explains this decline is the gradual opening up of Kurdistan to the outside world, with improved communications and the arrival of industrial products from Europe, competing with local production. Craft industries have either disappeared from many towns or have adapted to new demands. Travelling salesmen go from village to village offering cheap industrial products.

Kurdistan has thus gone from a traditional economy to an under-developed one, with a marked dependence on foreign industrial goods. The economic life of Kurdistan is sluggish because of the lack of industrialisation and poor communication routes, often constructed according to strategic rather than economic objectives. Asphalted roads are uncommon and journeys over short distances take a long time; it is often easier to get to a distant large town than it is to get to a neighbouring village just a few dozen kilometres away.

Kurdish is a language of the Iranian group and includes the dialects: Kurmanji (Turkey), Zaza (Turkey) and also Sorani (Iraq), which is not easily understood by Kurmanji speaking Kurds. Some communities speak Gurani (Iraq).

Apart from some assimilated groups, the Kurds express themselves in their own language and some of them know no other. The existence of two alphabets (Latin in Turkey, Arabic elsewhere) creates a barrier between the different Kurdish communities.

The religious factor amongst the Kurds

Most Kurds are *Sunni* of the *Shafi'i* school. This distinguishes them from their Arab and Turkish neighbours who are, in general, of the *Hanafi* school, or from the Turkish Azeris and the Persians who are *Shi'ites*.

In Turkey there are also Kurds who subscribe to a non-orthodox form of *Shi'ism*: the Alevis (Disciples of Ali). Many speak the Zaza dialect. In Kermanshah and Khanaqin, several tribes are orthodox *Shi'ites*, but some, to the west of Kermanshah and in Kirkuk, belong to the Ahl al Haqq sect (People of the Truth). It is possible that the Ahl al Haqqs originally came from the Ismaili sect, and their cult has many differences from orthodox (twelver) *Shi'ism*. The Yazidis practise a syncretist religion marked by a strong Ismaili influence. Referred to perjoratively as *Sheitanparast* (devil-worshippers) by their neighbours, the Yazidis maintain better relations with the Christians than with the Moslems. The Yazidis are for the most part settled to the south-west of Mosul, near the shrine of Shaikh Adi. Persecuted in the first half of the 19th century, they established themselves in the Caucasus, which then became the main centre of their community. More recently, a number of Turkish and Iraqi Yazidis have fled from the persecutions of the Moslem majority and settled in Germany.

Traditionally, the Christian and Jewish communities had an inferior status, and the protection given to the Christians by the western powers (Russia and Great Britain) provided an excuse for massacres, often instigated by the Sublime Porte.

The attacks on the Christian communities took a dramatic turn in 1915 with the deportation and massacres of Armenians organised by the government of the 'Young Turks' with the active complicity of certain Kurdish tribes. The persecution spread to other Christian communities (Jacobite, Assyrian and Nestorian), causing an exodus towards Iraq and Syria which were then under British and French mandate.

The Assyrian community rose up against the Iraqi government in 1933 in a bid to obtain autonomous status. The repression was brutal and the Patriarch was exiled.

In the *Sunni* and *Shi'ite* world, the *sada*,[1] theoretical descendants of the Prophet, enjoy a privileged status because of their ancestor Muhammad. Among the Kurds, the *sada* usually do not have much influence. The *sada* are an endogamous group but do not constitute a social class; they can be rich or poor. In the former case, the prestige of the individual is strengthened by his birth. For example the *shaikhs* of the *Qadiri* brotherhood, almost all of them *sada*, are considered by their disciples to be superior to others because of their birth. The fact of being a *sayyid* can equally increase the prestige of a tribal chief facing up to his rivals, even if this aspect has been watered down by the rise of nationalist feeling in the 20th century.

Under the Ottoman Empire, the *mufti* formed a religious hierarchy that ensured respect for the *sharia* (Koranic law). They could issue *fatwas* (religious decrees) which were legally valid. Dependant on the government of the caliphate or the local emir, the *mufti* did not play an important role in Kurdish political movements. The abolition of the caliphate in 1924 resulted in their becoming public servants and brought their influence to an end.

At the village level, the *mullahs* represent religious autonomy. They teach the children the basics of the Koran and conduct religious ceremonies. For a long time the *mullahs* were the principal guardians of classical culture, poetry, theology and literature, and it is only with the advent of state schools that their power began to decline.

Even a rapid account of the religious factor amongst the Kurds would be incomplete without mentioning the existence of the *Sufi* brotherhoods which play an important social and political role. As in all tribal societies, certain individuals, because they have a source of legitimacy outside the tribe, achieve positions of power by transcending, if only temporarily, the divisions between clans. It is therefore no coincidence that the late Mullah Mustafa Barzani, the most famous of the Kurdish leaders in Iraq, or his rival Jalal Talabani, come from religious families. They owe their influence in part to this fact.

The *shaikhs*, at the head of a *Sufi* brotherhood, are the objects of popular reverence which gives them considerable influence. They often serve as mediators in conflicts between groups, and their networks of disciples give them the capacity to mobilise large sections of the population, which explains their political clout.

All the *shaikhs* belong to the two *Sufi* orders represented amongst the Kurds: the *Qadiri* and *Naqshbandi*. The *Sufi* orders are independent of the tribes, independent of any state, and function like a secret society. There is no strict centralisation and several regional centres can co-exist.

The *shaikhs'* wealth is linked to their supposed healing powers and, more generally, to the grace (*baraka*) given to them by God. Disciples who come to see their master are expected to bring gifts. Furthermore, *shaikhs* who own domains can, because of their status, insist on additional services to which the aghas have no right. The social standing of the *shaikhs* also allows them to make tribal alliances by marriage, which strengthens their political and economic power. The harshness of relations between the *shaikhs* and their peasants has sometimes led to revolts.

The recruitment of *Sufi* disciples takes place mostly from the lower classes of society. These organisations are often the only ones open to the most disadvantaged, and may be used by the Kurdish nationalist networks.

The *Qadiri* order was named after Abd al-Qadir (1077-1166) who was not himself a *Sufi* master despite having received *Sufi* training. The earliest accounts presenting him as a saint did not appear until a century and a half after his death, and it was only in the 15th century that the order expanded throughout the Moslem world. It remained the only order in Kurdistan until the 19th century, and retains a strong presence.

The *Naqshbandi* order, founded in the 13th century, derives its name from Baha al-Din (1318-1359) who reformed it. The brotherhood was introduced into Kurdistan much later, at the beginning of the 19th century, by Mawlana Khalid, a Kurd of the Jaf tribe, who succeeded in establishing his order thanks to his talents as a preacher.

The situation of the Kurdish regions of the Ottoman Empire at the beginning of the 19th century also explains the expansion of the *Naqshbandi*. The penetration of European imperialism, in this instance British, and the activities of missionaries naturally provoked reactions of mistrust amongst the Moslem populations. The anti-Christian and anti-Western message of the *Sufi Naqshbandi* brotherhood was very much in tune with the feelings of the population. Meanwhile, the Kurdish emirates, which had until then maintained their autonomy, were progressively supplanted by the Ottoman administration's programme of reforms and centralisation under Mahmud II (1808-1839). The Kurdish emirates were reduced. The last, that of the Bedir Khan, led an important revolt against the centralisation of the Sublime Porte until the mid 19th century.

The arrival of Mawlana Khalid in 1808, before the emirates had disappeared, did not result in an immediate or vigorous expansion of his brotherhood. It was the next generation, confronted directly by the pressure for centralisation and by the decline of the emirs, which proved much more receptive. The influence of the *shaikhs* increased further as the Kurdish tribes, no longer subject to the authority of the emirs, constantly fought each other, necessitating arbitration by the *shaikhs*.

The *shaikhs* themselves, after having been at the heart of most of the Kurdish rebellious movements from the end of the 19th century until the 1920s, eventually saw their own influence decline. In Turkey, the Istanbul government's policy was to put under house arrest, or to exile, a number of *shaikhs*, and the considerable influence of the brotherhoods seemed no more than a memory until the political liberalisation in Turkey during the 1950s gave evidence of the durability of the phenomenon. The *shaikhs*, many having become city dwellers, then played an important political role, notably as members of the Democratic Party.

In Syria, the influence of the *shaikhs* remained unchanged until the 1950s, even increasing with the arrival of the displaced *shaikhs* from Turkey (in the 1920s). In the absence of any persecution, the *shaikhs'* loss of influence over the last three decades is attributable to the social and economic changes undergone by Syria. The rise of Kurdish nationalism, as a reaction to the Arabism personified by Nasser, was another factor damaging to the *shaikhs,* whose power is legitimised in relation to the Moslem world as a whole.

More generally, the weakening of the *shaikhs* is connected to the detribalisation which has affected the whole of Kurdish society. The easing of tribal conflicts reduces the role of the *shaikhs* as negotiators. In Iraq, for example, the nationalist movement has had sufficient influence over the past two or three decades to resolve conflicts, and in so doing play the role which traditionally fell to the *shaikhs*.

Finally, it is important to note the existence of a fundamentalist movement linked to the *Naqshbandi* order, and which is called in Turkish *Nurculuk* (Disciples of the Divine Light). This movement gained importance particularly after the Second World War and is at the moment a significant element within the fundamentalist movement in Turkey. The prime mover in *Nurculuk* was Said Nursi, a *mullah* born in 1873 in the province of Bitlis. In 1920 he sided with Mustafa Kemal, rather than with the Caliph, probably out of opposition to the western powers, but he later confronted the Kemalists despite many periods of imprisonment.

A collection of his essays was published in 1950, at the time of the liberalisation of the regime. In this text, *Risale-i Nur* (Treaty of the Divine Light), he explains the necessity of a return to a purified Islam. Expressing an extreme traditionalism, he violently attacks communists, western influence and non-orthodox sects such as the Alevis.

The tribe

The main characteristic of the social organisation of the Kurds is its great variety of forms. Tribal segmentation does, however, dominate the whole of society, since even those who are not tribalised are subject to its rules.

Amongst the Kurds, the tribe is a territorially-fixed social and economic unit, founded on real or imaginary blood ties which give the group its structure. The tribe is subdivided into subsystems down to the level of the clan, which is the cornerstone of the social system. The clan is an extended family defined by a common ancestor, even if genealogy appears to be a much lesser concern for the Kurds than it is for other tribal societies. In fact it is possible for an outsider to be adopted by a clan and for his descendants to be completely assimilated after only a few generations. A clan can even succeed, by virtue of its military or political gains, in absorbing another clan and in creating a common genealogy from the different pieces.

The basic unit from an economic point of view is the family. This is normally a nuclear family of parents and non-married children, although it is fairly common for a young married man to stay with his parents. There is also a tendency amongst wealthy landowners to keep their possessions undivided to avoid dispersion. A tribe would normally have begun by being in possession of its own territory, to which it would often have given its name. Even though the intrusion of state law has led to the suppression of the notion of purely tribal ownership of land, some examples do still exist. According to the anthropologist Martin van Bruinessen, a number of armed conflicts broke out in 1976 on the Batman plain after a member of the Reshkotan tribe sold land to an outsider. Grazing rights belong to the tribe collectively and particular areas are allotted to each clan. Nomadic tribes must pay a tax to the chief of the tribe that owns the land that is being crossed. This does not exclude recurrent conflicts, of course. However, the tribal chief who receives the tax does not redistribute it amongst the other members of the group, a beginning of private appropriation of land.

The pasture land around a village is communal property: for the sedentary population the village is the pivotal territorial unit, while for the state it serves as an administrative centre. Sometimes, the village community sometimes corresponds to a particular clan, to which 'outsiders' have become attached. On the other hand, village structures can often be more complicated, consisting of a number of unrelated clans. This can be a source of conflicts.

In Kurdish society, the limits of the tribe are not clearly defined. There is a nucleus of families that clearly belong to the same lineage. Individuals or groups, sometimes in numbers greater than the original village, will attach themselves to the nucleus, but may leave at a moment's notice, depending on the good or bad luck of their adopted village. Tribes can also disappear or come into existence relatively quickly. The one constant, the one important occasion when a tribe or a clan will always act as such, is a confrontation with another tribe or clan. In this sense, one could say that only conflict or revenge, which are essential aspects of tribal values, give this type of segmentary social organisation any relevance.

Revenge is between groups. The goal is not to punish the guilty individual, but the group to which he belongs. The cycle of revenge thus unleashed can last decades or even longer. Even today, in the remotest parts of Turkey, where the police has little or no presence, this type of conflict continues to exist. The non-tribal Kurds, along with non-tribal Christians who in the past did not have the right to carry arms, depend for their protection on tribal chiefs, who in return expect allegiance and subordination.

In the case of a murder, a sum of money can be given to the father, or by default, the brothers of the victim. The sum will vary according to the social position of the victim and of the murderer as well as the importance of the latter's clan. The penance is paid by the whole of the clan, even if it is a symbolic participation. This underlines the collective aspect of the responsibility. Such arrangements, generally the result of mediation, defuse the cycle of revenge. They are much easier to establish if the links of the group in conflict are close, since someone with the necessary authority, such as the chief of the tribe, can then be found. In the case of a conflict between two tribes, the mediator has to be the chief of another tribe who is neutral and has sufficient influence. This is rare since the tribes are reluctant to let a rival profit from their differences. As in most tribal societies, *shaikhs* often play the role of mediator. This also explains why the most influential tribal chiefs take pride in their external origins, which allow them to remain outside the web of tribal solidarity and therefore to mediate and arbitrate.

Attempts by governments to put a stop to the tribal system of private revenge and thereby to the influence of the *shaikhs* have met with mixed success. The Turkish government, having eliminated the traditional mediators, sometimes uses force to impose a solution, but the lack of any authority capable of legitimately proposing a compromise means that tension or confrontation still subsist within the villages.

Marriage reinforces tribal segmentation and increases the risk of conflict between groups. Therefore the type of marriage which, in theory, is preferred is that which unites a young man with the daughter of his paternal uncle. Custom provides a kind of priority for this type of marriage which cannot easily be refused and involves a smaller dowry. Apart from such marriages, preference is given to a close member of the family since this will have the effect of strengthening the cohesion of the clan.

The tribe is, in practice, the largest grouping within traditional Kurdish society. There has never been, at least up until the mid 20th century, any real national feeling capable of transcending tribal oppositions. Even in the 20th century, Kurdish nationalist movements have been systematically opposed, not only by governments, but also by government-allied Kurdish militias who have sought thereby to weaken a rival. Until recently, nationalism has never been a strong enough ideology to bridge such gulfs.

Unity within a tribe is not necessarily complete, even in the case of a conflict with another tribe. External allies are constantly called on by Kurdish chiefs seeking a decisive advantage. It is thus relatively easy for an external force to interfere in tribal affairs and even to secure nominal supremacy. Nevertheless, the play between the tribes is one of perpetual opposition. This excludes any strategic external alliance. The preferred op-tion is a series of manoeuvres aimed more at weakening rather than destroying an enemy. Allegiances can therefore fluctuate, but division itself, as a ground rule, remains a constant. As governments have increasingly intervened, claiming a monopoly on violence, the power bases of the tribal leaders have changed. Traditionally, a leader could hope to gain influence either through a war against other tribes or by mediation. Now, tribal leaders are forced to turn to the ever growing presence of the state to guarantee their power. The ability of these leaders to develop good relations with the authorities will increasingly become the key factor in determining their political successes or failures.

Kurdish dignitaries are essentially divided into two types: the agha is a tribal and therefore rural figure, traditionally the leader of a group of warriors; the beg is a city dwelling landlord, not necessarily of tribal origin, with tenant farmers to cultivate his lands.

The most significant social function for an agha is the provision of hospitality for passing travellers. The agha's income gives him the means to feed and house visitors in the guest-house. He thereby represents his village to the outer world. His generosity is one element of his status and his influence depends on it. The room used to receive outsiders is normally the *diwan* (literally the 'court'), the village parliament where communal activities (entertainments, the settling of disputes, etc.) are held. This allows the agha, who owns the *diwan*, to maintain it under his control. Over the past twenty years, the *diwans* have become less frequented and have lost much of their importance in everyday life. Traditionally, villagers were expected to attend the *diwan* once a month. Each member of the community, particularly the young, could have their behaviour publicly criticised without a right of reply. Apart from this aspect of social control, the *diwan* was also a meeting place where the agha would arrange for singers to perform or where games could be played.

The *diwans* went into decline during the 1960s. With the exception of Syria, where the government had them closed as a measure against the nationalist movement, their drop in popularity was caused by rapid social changes. The mechanisation introduced in the 1950s made the aghas less dependent on tenant farmers. These were often replaced by agricultural labourers, usually working on a seasonal basis and therefore village outsiders. Some aghas, having accumulated sufficient assets, eventually moved into town, and the *diwan* would be abandoned as a result.

To pay the costs involved in providing hospitality for outsiders, the aghas levied a tax from the villagers. This would usually amount to a 10 per cent share of the cereal crop or a fortieth of every flock. There was no *a priori* link between this tax and a tenancy, only with the agha's function as village representative. Nevertheless this 10 per cent tax is sometimes called 'rent' or even *zakat* (an alms tax, legal in Islamic law and destined for redistribution among the poor). This fluctuating terminology shows that in many cases it is not a popular tax and is sometimes collected under duress. During the last two decades, these practices have largely fallen into disuse and it is therefore noteworthy that nationalist organisations sometimes now collect these taxes instead of the aghas.

Not all Kurds are members of a clan or a tribe. Many live as dependants of tribal chiefs and in practice do not own any land, working as labourers or tenant farmers. Since the most brutal forms of exploitation of non-tribal Kurds have disappeared, the distinction between the two categories, which was once very clear, has become somewhat blurred. The situation has changed from one where non-tribal Kurds were, in some cases, sold with the land to one of a more limited form of economic exploitation. These non-tribal Kurds were either tribal individuals who had become sedentarised or else non-Kurds who had been gradually assimilated.

A brief history of the Kurds

The foundations

The ethnogenesis of the Kurds has been the subject of several hypotheses. For some, the Kurds are a people of Iranian origin who moved from the region of Urmiya to Botan in the 7th century BC. For others they are autochthonous. Xenophon, it is believed, mentions them in Anabasis under the name of 'Carduqi'. Whatever the case may be, their language is part of the Iranian group.

The history of the Kurds begins in a more verifiable way with the Arab conquest. Although their Islamicisation was rapid, this did not stop them from taking the lead in numerous rebellions against the conquering Arabs. Nevertheless the Kurdish dynasties were quickly eliminated to the advantage of the Seljuks and while the word 'Kurd' was used as early as the 7th century, the word 'Kurdistan' was used for the first time in the 12th century, when the Turkish Seljuk prince Sandjar created a province called Kurdistan with Bahar as its capital.

The Mongol invasion in the 12th century was the beginning of a period of withdrawal for the Kurds, who took almost no part in the conflicts between the Mongols, Arabs and Christians. The Turkish dynasties that supplanted the Mongols exerted their dominance over the Kurds, drawing them into the conflicts between the *Shi'ites* and the *Sunnis*. It was during this period that the Kurds of Sulaymaniya in Iraq moved to Lake Urmiya in Iran.

At the beginning of the 16th century there was a Kurdish revival, brought about by the opposition between the Ottomans and the powerful Safavids in Iran. The Persians were defeated by the Turks at the battle of Chaldiran in 1514. From then on, the majority of Kurds were part of the Ottoman Empire. Now under Ottoman rule, which was more liberal than that of the Shah of Iran, the Kurdish marches were reorganised into semi-independent principalities by Sultan Selim's minister, Hakim Idris, prince of Bitlis, who was himself a Kurd. This belt of principalities allowed the Kurds to stop the Persian advance. The treaty of 1639 between Persia and the Sublime Porte recognised this by fixing frontiers between the two states which remained valid right up until the 19th century.

The organisation of the Kurdish emirates was broadly similar to that of the Ottoman state, but its administrative integration remained very weak. The emir kept the bulk of the taxes collected for himself and sent only a small portion to the sultan in Constantinople. The emir would also put only part of his military forces at the sultan's disposal. Similarly, justice was administered by a *qadi* dependent on the emir rather than on the sultan. The Sublime Porte tolerated this degree of independence, to a much greater extent than usual, because of the frontier position of the emirates and the mountainous geography of the region. These two factors meant that political control could be achieved only by consent and the Sublime Porte therefore accepted compromises. With their position thus assured, the emirs were able to preserve a large part of their autonomy until the beginning of the 19th century.

The rebellions of the 19th century

The policy of centralisation undertaken by the Sublime Porte during the course of the first half of the 19th century, provoked a series of rebellious movements in the Kurdish emirates. The first major insurrection broke out in 1806, in the principality of Baban. Founded in the 16th century, this principality had played a decisive role in the 17th and 18th centuries and had expanded considerably. After the death of Ibrahim Pasha Bebe, chief of the tribe and founder of Sulaymaniya (Iraq), the Ottoman government decided to smash the power of the Baban. First of all the Sublime Porte attempted to impose a successor to Ibrahim Pasha, chosen from outside the tribe. The latter's nephew, Abdurrahman Pasha, then launched a guerilla campaign against the Turkish forces and a number of Kurdish tribes who had rallied to their cause. This lasted three years before Abdurrahman Pasha, finally defeated, took refuge in Iran at the end of 1808.

The 1830s were marked by another uprising, led by Mir Muhammad, sovereign of the principality of Soran. In 1833 from his base in Riwanduz and at the head of an army of 10,000 horsemen and 20,000 infantrymen, Mir Muhammad was able to impose his authority over the whole of southern Kurdistan but was unable to forge an alliance with the emir of Botan. The sultan, concerned by Mir Muhammad's progress, dispatched troops from Sivas, Mosul and Baghdad. The engagements of the summer of 1834 were extremely violent and the Ottoman troops had to retreat without having gained any decisive advantage. Mir Muhammad took advantage of this respite, conquering Iranian Kurdistan. Despite his attempts to win over the Iranian government by recognising Persian sovereignty, the emir found himself alone when faced with a fresh Ottoman offensive during the summer of 1836. The 40,000 men defending Riwanduz beat off the Ottoman army. The commander of the Sultan's troops then made an appeal to the religious feelings of the population and a Kurdish *mullah*, Mullah Khati issued a *fatwa* forbidding the struggle against the caliph. This had the effect of shattering the Kurdish resistance and Mir Muhammad was forced to surrender. Taken to Constantinople, he was received by the Sultan, who had him assassinated a year later.

The revolt led by the emir of Botan, Bedr Khan Beg, began in 1840. In the first years of his reign, Bedr Khan Beg, who had been emir since 1821, organised a well disciplined regular army. Following the Ottoman defeat at Nizib, he managed to seize a large part of the Ottoman Empire's Kurdish territories. A believer in the freedom of worship, the emir treated Christians and Jews with respect. Furthermore, as a good administrator, he imposed order on the territories he controlled, in marked and happy contrast to the anarchy of the Ottoman administration.

Nevertheless, confrontation with the Ottoman army, from 1844 onwards, was to reveal the emirate's weaknesses. At the Sultan's request, English and American missionaries had brought their influence to bear on the Christians, who refused to fight against the Ottoman troops. Worse still Bedr Khan Beg's own nephew betrayed him. After continuing to resist for a while longer, Bedr Khan Beg capitulated and died an exile in Damascus in 1868.

The Crimean War of 1853 provided Yezdan Sher with an opportunity to carry out his plan for an independent Kurdistan, with himself as king. The uprising began in 1855 with the capture of Bitlis by 2,000 warriors. In the same offensive, he conquered Mosul and its arsenal, enough to equip 30,000 men. This small army was then aimed at Siirt, a strategic position on the Ottoman eastern flank. Success followed success.

The winter of 1855 and the withdrawal of the Russian forces left the Sublime Porte free to put down the Kurdish revolt, but this proved unnecessary, as forces led by Yezdan Sher soon disintegrated. The decisive factor turned out to be the steps taken by British diplomats, committed to the cause of the Ottoman Empire in the war against Russia. A British emissary was received by Yezdan Sher and took the opportunity to buy off some tribal chiefs who soon refused to fight. Deceived by the promises of the British, Yezdan Sher set off to negotiate in Constantinople, where he was imprisoned.

Shaikh Ubaydallah's rebellion was that of a religious rather than a tribal leader. Head of the *Naqshbandi* brotherhood, Ubaydallah clashed with the

Iranian government in 1872 after it reopened the question of a tax concession which had been granted by the Shah in 1836. An Ottoman emissary conveyed Ubaydallah's protests, but to no effect; the population was obliged to pay the tax to the Iranian government, rather than to the *shaikh*, as in the past.

The final break occurred after the 1877-1878 war between Russia and Turkey in which the *shaikh* took part. The famines caused by the fighting and the corruption of the Ottoman administration persuaded him to rebel. After seeking support from the *sharif* of Mecca and the *khedive* of Egypt, Shaikh Ubaydallah turned first to Russia, unsuccessfully, then to Britain. The British provided the insurgents with arms and ammunition and the Ottoman government, hoping that Ubaydallah would move against Iran, decided not to interfere. The offensive against Iran began in the summer of 1880. The Kurdish towns of Mahabad and Miandobad were taken. But, instead of marching on Tabriz, the Kurdish troops took to looting. The Shah of Iran had little difficulty convincing the Sultan that the existence of such a sizeable Kurdish movement constituted a threat to them both. Faced with the combined strength of the Iranian and Turkish troops, Shaikh Ubaydallah was forced to pull out of Iran. Following a period of house arrest in Constantinople, he ended up, after a last fruitless attempt in 1882 to gain backing from Russia, in exile in Mecca.

The birth of Kurdish nationalism

A sense of Kurdish identity can already be found in the work of the poet Ahmad Khani, a central figure in Kurdish literary culture whose popularity has never waned. However, until the 20th century, the only model of unification for the Kurds remained membership of a movement instigated by a charismatic figure, a movement which would collapse the moment he disappeared.

In the 19th century, Kurdish nationalism thus initially manifested itself in attempts to establish principalities independent of central government (whether Ottoman or Persian). The gap left by the disappearance of the independent emirates during the first half of the 19th century was filled by new political leaders: the *shaikhs* who, from then on, were to be found at the head of all the important rebellions. With their far from negligible social base amongst the peasants, the movements led by the *shaikhs* had a resonance which was at once patriotic and messianic. These ill fated insurrections combined to produce a sense of Kurdish identity, a prelude to the development of modern nationalism in the 20th century which remained characterised by the presence of leaders at its head issued from the great *shaikh* families (the Barzanis and the Talabanis), who could capitalise on ancestral allegiances as well as ancient enmities. By and large, the Kurdish national movement was to find itself unable to overcome the segmentation of society, and its nationalist parties were always weakened and undermined by divisions.

The idea of a Kurdish nation is a relatively recent one and is ultimately linked to the abandonment of the Moslem concept of the *ummah*. Like the Turks, the great majority of Kurds were *Sunnis* and felt some affinity with the caliphate, all the more so because of the way Sultan Abdul Hamid II (1876-1908) skilfully played on this solidarity and associated the Kurds with the government through the intermediary of the *Hamidiye* militias.

In 1891, Sultan Abdulhamid had created a tribal militia named the *Hamidiye*. It was led by tribal chiefs and its purpose was to insure the Sultan's control over the eastern provinces of the empire. This resulted in a reaffirmation of the authority of the tribal leaders and also allowed some of them to increase their influence.

The Sultan's policy, which was to guarantee the security of the region against the Armenians and to secure personal loyalties, was crowned with success. The *Hamidiye* played an important role in the Armenian massacres of 1895 to 1896. Officially disbanded with the coming to power of the Young Turks in 1908, the tribal regiments were recreated a little later as militias and fought in the Balkan war of 1912-13.

Nationalism, a European idea born at the end of the 18th century with the French revolution, made its appearance in the educated circles of Ottoman society during the 1880s. *Kurdistan*, the first Kurdish newspaper, was founded in 1898 by Mihad Bedir Khan Bey. It was a bilingual publication in Turkish and Kurdish, appearing in response to prevailing political circumstances. It was first published in Europe and then in Cairo during the First World War. A society for the 'Recovery and Progress of Kurdistan' was formed in 1908 and its organisers included General Sharif Pasha and the son of Shaikh Ubaydallah. At the same time the promising beginnings of a Kurdish committee for the propagation of education were spoiled by rivalries amongst its organisers. The Young Turk revolution of 1908, which saw itself as liberal and founded on an Ottomanism open to the diverse communities of the empire, soon fell into pan-Turk ultra-nationalism.

In Kurdistan itself, young nationalists gathered together in Kurdish clubs in Bitlis, Mus, Diyarbakir, Erzurum and Mosul. But the advance of the Kurdish movement was interrupted by the repressive measures taken by the Young Turks beginning in 1909. Its principal leaders were imprisoned or executed. This was a fertile period for Kurdish uprisings, but also for Arab or Armenian ones.. A reversal of the Young Turks' policy permitted the legalisation of *Hiviya Kurd* (Kurdish Hope) which until then had been a secret society. Under the leadership of Khalil Hassan Mokti, who was later to champion Turkish assimilationist theses, the movement published a journal: *Roja Kurd* (Kurdish Day).

Notes

1. Plural of *sayyid*, theoretically, a descendant of the Prophet.

2. The Kurds of Turkey

Official ideology: the Kemalist model

Turkey's official ideology has remained fundamentally unchanged since Mustafa Kemal, the founder of modern Turkey. The Ottoman Empire's traditional model of integration was based on an organisation into *millets*, religious communities largely managed by the churches (Armenian, Assyrian, Greek or Jewish). The break came under Abdul Hamid II (1876-1908), whose pan-Islamic policy led to worsening inter-religious and nationalist conflicts, notably the first Armenian massacres in 1895-96. Turkish nationalist sentiments started to emerge during the 1880s. Despite their initial collaboration with the minorities, particularly the Armenians, the coming to power of the Young Turks in 1908 marked the beginning of the domination of nationalist ideology in Turkey.

During the post-war period, the Kemalists inherited much of the Young Turks anti-Armenian policy. Their attitude towards the Kurds was, at the outset, rather ambiguous. After the expulsion of the Greeks and the mass extermination of the Armenians, the Kurds were the only remaining important non-Turkish element in the country. The traditional policy of the Ottoman state was to strengthen its rule over the Kurdish territories rather than the 'turkisation' of the Kurdish population.

Between 1919 and 1923, the Kemalists seemed to be following the same attitude, but this was a purely tactical alliance for the Kemalists. It allowed Turkey to maintain six *vilayets* populated mainly by Kurds but claimed by the Armenians. Indeed, Mustafa Kemal's first political victory at the congress of Erzurum (July-August 1919), which was attended by 54 delegates from the five Kurdish *vilayets* of Erzurum, Bitlis, Van, Mus and Erzincan, was the passage of a resonantly pan-Islamic anti-Armenian programme.

The Kurds participated extensively in the war against Greece, when the latter invaded Anatolia. On the 1st of November 1922, once military victory was assured, Mustafa Kemal declared to Parliament: 'The state is a Turkish state'. Repression directed against the Kurds, the only community which threatened the existence of Turkey as a quasi ethnically homogenous nation state, soon followed.

The suppression of the caliphate in 1924, the attacks against Islam when it attempted to become political, destroyed the bonds which tied the Kurds to the central state. Kurdish nationalism, at times tinged with religious fervour, prospered in the backlash. The clergy supported the Kurdish movements as opponents of secular Kemalism. The rapid and vigorous westernisation required by Kemalist modernisation clashed with the traditional structures of Kurdish society.

Mustafa Kemal Atatürk's plan for devising a nation led him to create a mythical history of Turkey, *ab nihilo*. The Turks, who originally came from central Asia, became the originators of the great Sumerian, Babylonian and Hittite civilisations of Asia Minor and Mesopotamia. In this hyper-nationalist vision, the Kurds simply do not exist. According to the Kemalist official historians the Kurds were originally Turanian and came from the steppes of central Asia five thousand years ago and their present dialect is a corruption of Turkish mixed with Persian and Arabic.

As late as 1961, General Gürsel, the leader of the junta that had taken power, maintained that the Kurds are of Turkish origin. The military, guardians of the sacred flame of Kemalism, have always showed themselves particularly resistant to any recognition of the Kurdish phenomenon. Until recently the euphemism 'Mountain Turks' was still in general use.

The legal measures used against the Kurds

The treaty of Lausanne of 24th July 1923 gave birth to modern Turkey. The signatories to the treaty, the British Empire, France, Italy, Japan, Romania, Serbia and Turkey, defined a legal framework for the country, the provisions of which are still valid today.

In particular, section III (articles 37-44) deals with the 'Protection of Minorities': 'No restrictions shall be imposed on the free use by any Turkish national of any language in private intercourse, in commerce, religion, in the press, or in publications of any kind or at public meetings. Notwithstanding the existence of the official language, adequate facilities shall be given to Turkish nationals of non-Turkish speech for the oral use of their own language before the Courts.' (article 39). However, these articles only concern the Jewish or Christian religious minorities.

During this period, 75 Kurdish deputies held seats in the Grand National Assembly at Ankara. Then, from March 1924, speaking or publishing in Kurdish were banned and the Constitution of the same year consecrated Mustafa Kemal's voluntarist fiction, according to which Turkey is strictly Turkish. The current Constitution, drawn up by the Consultative Assembly after the military *coup d'état* of 12th September 1980, states in its preamble: 'The determination that no protection shall be afforded to thoughts or opinions contrary to Turkish national interests, the principle of the existence of Turkey as an indivisible entity with its state and territory, Turkish historical and moral values, or the nationalism, principles, reforms and modernism of Atatürk'. Continuity with the thinking of the founder of modern Turkey as well as the refusal to recognise Kurdish cultural identity were reaffirmed.

Two articles in the Constitution prohibited the Kurdish language and its written dissemination, without actually naming it.

Article 26 states 'Everyone has the right to express and disseminate his thought and opinion by speech, in writing or in pictures or through other media, individually or collectively ... No language prohibited by law shall be used in the expression and dissemination of thought. Any written or printed documents, phonograph records, magnetic or video tapes, and other means of expression used in contravention of this provision shall be seized by a duly issued decision of judge or, in cases where delay is deemed prejudicial, by the competent authority designated by law.'

Article 28 states 'The Press is free and shall not be censored. The establishment of a printing house shall not be subject to prior permission and to the deposit of a financial guarantee. Publication shall not be made in any language prohibited by law. The state shall take the necessary measures to ensure the freedom of the Press and freedom of information. In the limitation of freedom of the Press, Articles 26 and 27 of the Constitution are applicable ...'

For the Kurds, the right of association was, in practice, banned by the law no.765 published in the official Journal of the Turkish republic on 3rd March 1926. Articles 141 and 142 contain the key provisions:

Article 141-4: 'Any attempt, on the basis of race, to suppress or eliminate the rights recognised by the Constitution, the creation or attempted creation of organisations aiming to weaken or diminish national sentiments, and the leadership or administration of such organisation are criminal offences punishable by from eight to fifteen years incarceration.'

141-5: 'Membership of such organisation is punishable by from five to twelve years incarceration.'

141-6: 'These terms of imprisonment will be increased by one third if the above-mentioned crimes are committed within government offices, town halls, schools or establishments for higher education, trade union or other labour organisations, buildings belonging to organisations whose capital is owned or partly owned by the state, and similarly if they are committed by employees and officials of such bodies.'

141-8: 'For the purposes of this legislation, an organisation shall consist of any gathering of two or more persons to pursue a common goal.'

Article 142-3: 'Any person who, on the basis of race, attempts to suppress or eliminate the rights recognised by the Constitution, or attempts to weaken or diminish national sentiments will be liable to a term of imprisonment of from five to ten years.'

142-4: 'Anyone found guilty of praising the above-mentioned actions will be liable to a term of imprisonment of from two to five years incarceration.'

142-5: 'These terms of imprisonment will be increased by one third if the above-mentioned crimes are committed in the circumstances laid down in article 141-6.'

142-6: 'If any of the above mentioned criminal offences is committed by way of publication, the sentences will be increased by one half.'

The right to form Kurdish political parties, an extension of the right of association, was banned by law no. 2820, concerning the status of political parties, published on 24th April 1983. Article 81: 'Political parties: a) cannot affirm that there exists on Turkish soil any minority founded on national, cultural, religious, sectarian, racial or linguistic differences; b) cannot have as its aim the sapping of national unity by the creation of minorities on the territory of the Turkish Republic through the protection, development and diffusion of any language or culture other than the Turkish language and culture; c) cannot use any language other than Turkish in the drawing up and publication of their programme and statutes, congresses, meetings, public gatherings and propaganda; nor may they use or diffuse any banners, records, posters, recordings, films, brochures and tracts in a language other than Turkish; nor may they remain indifferent to actions of this kind committed by others. However, they may translate their statutes and programme into foreign languages other than those that are forbidden by law.'

This provision was strengthened by another law, no. 2392, relating to publications in languages other than Turkish, published on 22nd October 1983. Article 2 in particular stipulates that 'it is forbidden to express, diffuse or publish opinions in any language other than the main official language of states recognised by the Turkish state... '

This provision is aimed at the Kurdish language which was recognised as the second official language of Iraq after the agreements of 11th March 1970. This article had the effect of banning the entry of any publication in Kurdish coming from Iraq.

Article 3 of this law goes straight to the heart of Kemalist logic: 'The mother tongue of Turkish citizens is Turkish. It is forbidden: a) to use as a mother tongue any language other than Turkish, and to engage in any activity aimed at the broadcasting of these languages; b) to carry, at public gatherings and assemblies, placards, banners, signs, boards, posters and the like, written in a language other than Turkish, even in those languages not forbidden by this law, and, unless authorisation has been obtained from the highest civil authority in the locality, to use discs, sound recordings, films and other mediums and means of expression and diffusion in these languages.'

Anyone contravening the law faces a sentence of between 6 months and 2 years in prison and a fine of at least 100,000 Turkish liras (article 4 of the same law).

A further sentence of between 5 and 10 years in prison can be imposed if article 142-3 of the penal code (see above) is breached.

In the same spirit, a governmental decree, no. 83/7006, published on 2nd December 1983, bans those films 'aiming to undermine national integrity and unity, by creating differences of language, race, religion or creed'.

This legislation has not yet been repealed. After the official declarations by Turkish leaders concerning 'the Kurdish reality' the recasting of this legislation should now be on the agenda.

Some examples of the application of the legislation

In 1966, Emin Bozarslan published an ABC for the Kurdish children of Turkey: the book was immediately banned.

In March 1973, Franz Reissig, a Lufthansa employee, was imprisoned after the word 'Kurdistan' appeared by mistake in one of the company's advertisements. Similarly, a team from the organisation *Médecins sans Frontières* spent five months in prison for possession of a cassette in Turkish and a document in French about the Kurds. In like manner, *Kurdish Music*, a record of traditional music brought out by UNESCO, is still banned in Turkey.

The exemplary case of the sociologist Ismail Besikçi (who is not of Kurdish descent) clearly highlights the absurdity of the existing repressive system. This Turkish scholar has spent more than ten years in prison for his writings on the Kurds. Born in 1939, Ismail Besikçi studied at the Faculty of Political Sciences of the University of Ankara. After having been posted to eastern Anatolia during his military service, he decided to devote his sociology thesis to the Kurds. It was published in 1969 under the title, *The Socio-Economic and Ethnic Foundations of Eastern Anatolia*. Despite the fact that his work did not excite any scientific debate, he was sacked from his post at the University of Erzurum and sent to prison for 'communist and Kurdish' propaganda. His first period of imprisonment, from 1971 to 1974, ended with the amnesty decreed by the new Turkish prime minister, Bulent Ecevit. Three publications on the Kurdish problem won him a second stay in prison, from 1979 to 1981. He was arrested again two months later for having sent a letter to the president of the Swiss Union of Writers in which he questioned the validity of official ideology concerning the Kurdish question. He remained in prison until May 1987. Ismail Besikçi has been adopted as a Prisoner of Conscience by Amnesty International.

The freedom of the press is also limited by legislation. The Turkish daily newspaper *Ileri Yurt* (The Progressive Country) first appeared in the autumn of 1958. It exposed the difficult situation in eastern Anatolia. In December 1959 the director of the publication was arrested along with fifty or so others.

In the mid 1970s, an attempt to publish a newspaper in Kurdish gained its proprietor a twelve year prison sentence. The newspaper *Roja Welat* was connected with the SPTK. The director of the publication and the journalist,

Mehmet Ali Birand, who had interviewed Abdullah Ocalan (Apo), the leader of the PKK, were prosecuted under article 142 of the Penal Code for 'anti-national propaganda'. Threatened with a fifteen year prison sentence, they were finally acquitted in 1989.

Since 1982, the government no longer accepts typically Kurdish names. For instance, on 6th May 1983, the court of justice at Agra banned two Kurdish names on the pretext that their adoption would affect the 'interests of the Turkish republic'.

Even politicians are not always safe from prosecution. In March 1981, Serafetin Elçi, ex-minister of public works in the Ecevit cabinet and ex-independent member for the Kurdish province of Mardin, received a prison sentence and was incarcerated from 1981 to 1984 for having declared, during a private meeting, that he was of Kurdish origin. A similar case is that of Mehdi Zana, who was elected as mayor of Diyarbakir in 1979. In 1980, the now ex-mayor of Turkey's foremost Kurdish town, began a prison sentence of thirty-two years and eight months. In February 1987, following a mission of the European Parliament and the International Federation of Human Rights, the sentence was reduced on appeal to twenty-six years. Mehdi Zana's crime was to have used Kurdish in the exercise of his functions as mayor. He was finally released in April 1991. On the other hand, the lawyer and member for Urfa, Kemal Badilli, took advantage of his parliamentary immunity to publish a Kurdish grammar.

The administration of the 'provinces of the East'

From the very beginning of the Kemalist era, the administrative system revealed what the official discourse denied. Exceptional measures, such as the tribunal for the independence of the *vilayets* of the East, were imposed at an early date. This itinerant tribunal, which had the right to impose capital sentences without the approval of the parliament in Ankara, was much criticised, particularly for its corruption. In practice its role was to stamp out any trace of opposition to the government's programme of modernisation.

Another significant factor was the militarisation of the administration in the eastern provinces. An inspectorate general was created at the end of the 1920s and two others a few years later. The inspector general, who was usually a military man, had the upper hand over the civilian administration. Appointed by Mustafa Kemal, he was not answerable to the National Assembly for his actions. There were also many *vilayets* created for military ends and run by officers. At that time the army had more than 50,000 men in eastern Anatolia and made the law there. In 1943, a general, accused of having 33 Kurds shot without trial, was acquitted under pressure from the army. According to the Turkish leadership, the army was the best possible instrument of integration, functioning as a 'melting pot of nationalities', as it was then believed to do in the USSR.

Today a prefect represents the supreme political and administrative authority. His powers were specified by a decree on 16th December 1990, an April decree of the same year having been invalidated by the Constitutional Court. The prefect has the right to ban publications, even without a previous decision of a tribunal, but a warning is necessary. He can also close down printing works for ten days, then thirty days if the offence is repeated (the previous decree allowed for an unlimited closure). The police can search houses and take the inhabitants to the police station for questioning. Finally, the prefect is still not legally accountable to parliament for his actions. Even after the liberalisation of the regime in the 1950s, militarisation continued to be an important factor. After 1966, specialised commandos conducted numerous police operations, surrounding villages and searching the inhabitants. Many witnesses have testified that the military engaged in rape, torture and the murder of civilians on these occasions.

With the 1971 military *coup d'état*, the supporters of a policy of repression were returned to power. From 1971 to 1973, the tribunal of the state of siege, which sat in Diyarbakir, imposed a variety of sentences on more than a thousand Kurds. After 1986, renewed PKK (Workers' Party of Kurdistan) infiltration and attacks provoked another burst of activity by the security forces — the army, the gendarmerie and the secret services — which continues to this day.

In part at least because of the Kurdish problem, the army has become one of the major factors of Turkish political life. The financial cost of the wars of the 1920s and 30s amounted to almost a quarter of the national budget. The Kurdish uprisings also led to the construction of strategic railway lines, (Ankara-Sivas and Fevzi-Pasa-Diyarbakir), under direct army control, enabling rapid deployment of troops.

In the last few years, the need to guard the frontiers and to stop infiltrations, principally by members of the PKK, has demanded huge investments. The border with Syria is protected by four lines of electrified barbed wire, with observation posts every 200 metres. Further to the east, the extremely mountainous terrain along the Iraqi frontier makes this sort of arrangement impossible. Patrols proved to be ineffective and therefore the government has set up militias. There are two or three of these guards per village, several thousand in total. They and their families are prime targets for PKK partisans. They are armed by the government and their duty is to prevent infiltrations. The fact remains that it is impossible to achieve control of the border without the co-operation of the neighbouring states.

Two policies have been pursued in Kurdistan since the 1920s: deportation and especially 'turkisation'. The policy of deportation began as early as 1927, soon after Shaikh Said of Piran's rebellion was brutally quelled. It apparently affected a considerable number of Kurds who were transferred to western Turkey. Up until 1934 the deportations had been carried out under the authority of the inspectorate general. In 1934 they were made official by a law regulating the implantation of Turkish culture and the deportation of Kurdish populations.

From the 1940s and 50s onwards, the deportations were to have more limited objectives. In 1980, for example, a law authorised the deportation of all the relatives of a political prisoner. In the same way, the government tried to empty strategic (frontier) zones. To achieve this, the prefect had the right to offer financial incentives to depopulate certain areas: 43 villages have been evacuated in return for financial compensations. Similarly, 50,000 inhabitants of the province of Kars near the Soviet border and peasants from villages situated near the Iraqi and Syrian borders have been displaced.

The policy of turkisation is conducted in the same systematic fashion.

Since before the war, the Ankara administration has often decreed the changing of the names of towns and villages. Recently, the Minister of the Interior changed the names of 12,861 of Turkey's 34,957 agglomerations; 80 per cent of these innovations occurred in eastern Turkey.

Initially, the government's real intermediary were the RPP (Republican People's Party), which had been belatedly introduced into Kurdistan, the 'Houses of the People' and the 'Turkish Centres', which spread the Kemalist ideology.

The policy of turkisation is a major factor in education, particularly in the towns; in the countryside, the proportion of children attending schools is relatively small in any case.

It is difficult to measure either the degree to which the Kurds have been assimilated, or the extent of turkisation. Although it is clear that urbanisation has been an important factor, it is also the case that the most nationalist Kurds seem to come from the towns.

The Kurdish rebellions in Turkey

This section deals with the rebellions that took place in Turkey between 1925 and 1938, in reaction to Kemalist policy. The state of tension that existed between the Kurds and central government at this time led to a period of marked instability. Three great rebellions shook eastern Anatolia and have left a lasting legacy.

Shaikh Said's revolt (February-April 1925)

The key figure of this uprising was a religious leader belonging to the *Naqshbandi* brotherhood. His spiritual influence, which was essential for the mobilisation of the tribal chiefs who were to take part in the revolt, contributed to the ambiguous meaning of this insurrection, which appeared to be both religious and nationalist.

His religious status allowed him to rally the principal Kurdish tribes. Islamic propaganda certainly played its part in his discourse, with some success amongst the Turkish troops which worried the government in Ankara. Shaikh Said was advocating a state based on the *sharia* (Koranic law).

The strategy adopted was of a direct attack on the principal towns. The aim was to install, without delay, an embryonic administration, a *de facto* state in order to gain international recognition. The initial successes and the sheer scale of the rebellion took the Kemalist government by surprise. More than 10,000 men and 23 planes were mobilised. The Kurdish defeat at Diyarbakir in March 1925 was a turning point Shaikh Said's partisans. They were forced to evacuate the towns and take refuge in the north-east. Some of the leaders went to Iran where they were welcomed by the Kurdish chief, Simko. Others were taken by the army and executed. Amongst these was Shaikh Said himself who was hung at Diyarbakir on 25th September 1825 along with 52 of his partisans. Special tribunals which had just been established condemned hundreds of Kurds as well as a few Turkish leaders accused of collusion with the separatists.

Despite the declarations of Turkish officials, there is no proof of any British implication in the revolt. On the contrary, it is notable that France, by authorising Turkish soldiers to make use of the railway in northern Syria, allowed the Ankaran forces to surround the Kurds who were besieging Diyarbakir and to strike a decisive blow against Shaikh Said's revolt.

Nevertheless, the movement had not yet been completely crushed. Some chieftains, such as Yado of Palu and Aliye Unis of Sasun, headed armed bands and managed to confront the Turkish troops and even inflict a few losses on them. This guerilla warfare led to reprisals in the form of deportations which resulted tens of thousands of deaths.

The Mount Ararat revolt (1930)

The retreat of the Kurdish fighters towards the north-east turned Ararat into an insecure zone where, from 1927, army convoys were systematically attacked.

Abroad, a national Kurdish league was formed in Lebanon and called *Hoybun* (Independence). The founding congress in 1927 brought together different Kurdish organisations in the presence of a Dashnak Armenian leader, Vahan Papazyan. *Hoybun*'s principal leaders belonged to the great 'feudal' (that is to say tribal) Kurdish families.

The Dashnak party, struggling against the Soviet annexation of Armenia, represented an opening towards the West (France and Great Britain). At the time, the choice of the Ararat region could be explained, in part, by this

Kurdo-Armenian alliance which, for a while, received the support of the Shah of Iran.

By 1920, General Ihsan Nuri Pasha, the leader of the Kurdish force, had already taken control of the area between Mount Ararat and the north of Van and Bitlis. Negotiations then took place with the Turkish government, which realised that the Kurdish nationalists were growing stronger. As a result Ankara organised troop concentrations in May 1930. Mobilisation was slow, possibly because of the political and social problems that were troubling Turkey at the time. In the end more than 65,000 men took part in the attack which was launched in June 1930.

The resistance of the Kurdish troops, with hundreds of Turkish prisoners taken and planes shot down, forced the Turkish government into an understanding with Iran. The Shah then suspended aid to the Kurds and allowed the Turkish forces free passage across his territory in order to take the Kurds from the rear. The military collapse was all the more inevitable since the leaders of the Ararat revolt were unable to involve the Iranian Kurds or even those from nearby Dersim.

The insurgents finally dispersed, some of them to seek refuge in Iran. The repression that followed was savage. A law published on 29th July 1931 stipulated that: 'Killings, and other acts committed, either individually or collectively, by representatives of the state or of its provinces, by civil or military personnel, as well as by local authorities, guards or the militia, or any civilian having aided them or having acted in accord with them, from the 20th June 1930 to the 10th December 1930, in the pursuit and the extermination of uprisings which took place at Ercis, Zilan, Agri Dagh [Ararat] and the surrounding area, also including the region of the first inspectorate and the district of Pulumur, in the province of Erzincan, will not be considered as crimes.' (Article 1).

The repression came down on all the Kurdish regions, not just those involved in the revolt. Mass deportation was organised by a law of 5th May 1932 which instituted four zones.

'No 1 zones comprise those regions where it is desired to increase the density of the populations having a Turkish culture.

'No 2 zones comprise those regions where it is desired to establish populations which require assimilation into the Turkish culture.

'No 3 zones comprise those territories where immigrants of Turkish culture may freely establish themselves, without the aid of the authorities [the most fertile of the Kurdish regions].

'No 4 zones comprise those territories which it is desired to evacuate, and which are prohibited areas, for medical, cultural, political, strategic and public order reasons [this last zone includes the least accessible Kurdish regions].'

In February 1932 a substantial number of Kurds were deported to Anatolia. These population transfers ended in 1935.

The Dersim revolt (1936-1938)

This particularly mountainous and inaccessible region had, until then, kept out of all the revolts. But it was also opposed to any collaboration with the central government (its inhabitants were not part of the *Hamidiye*).

In the 1930s, the Kemalist policy towards Dersim was remarkably ambiguous. Threats of military action alternated with negotiations in Ankara with Dersim's leaders. In the context of the 1932 law on accommodation, Dersim belonged to the fourth category, that is one to be totally evacuated. In 1936, an attempt to transfer the population provoked a categorical refusal. Even though 60,000 soldiers took part in the operations, the resistance, made easier by the terrain, was long and bitter. There was no appeasement until October 1938 and the region was left devastated and prohibited to foreigners, like all of the Kurdish east, until 1965.

The violence of the repression smashed the Kurdish movement which was not rebuilt until the liberalisation of the 1950s.

The defeat of the Kurdish movements in the 1920s and 30s had both external and internal causes. One of the foremost of these was the fact that Kemalist ideology provided the state an intellectual framework and a capacity for mobilisation strengthened by an ancient administrative and military tradition. Also, the great powers, France anxious to please Turkey, Britain not wishing to destabilise Iraq, remained deaf to Kurdish demands. As far as the Kurds were concerned, Iran shared the same interests as Turkey. This materialised when territories were exchanged at the time of the treaty of 1932.

Compared to that of the Turks and the Armenians, Kurdish nationalism was something of a latecomer and at that time failed to produce any modernist elites to run the national movement. The absence of a strong national feeling at the community level prevented the revolts from spreading. In a segmented society, local solidarities retain more importance than a nationalist ideal.

Social conditions in the Kurdish regions

Demography

A demographic evaluation of the Kurds of Turkey is not without its difficulties. The 1965 census, the last to include the question of language, probably underestimated the number of Kurds, particularly those who were living in Turkish towns and who were afraid of affirming their identity.

The lowest estimates, for example those of the CIA for 1979, give a figure of some 4 to 6 million Kurds for that year. The press has occasionally noted a population of more than 8 million for the year 1989. On the other hand, Kendal Nezan has put forward the figure of 12 million Kurds for 1987, or some 24 per cent of the total population of 52 million inhabitants. Finally, Van Bruinessen's figure for 1975 is 7.5 million Kurds (Van Bruinessen, 1978, p.22). One of the factors that might explain these discrepancies is the presence of a large Kurdish population outside of Kurdistan which may or may not be considered to be in the process of being assimilated. Ozal, Turkey's head of state, has cited the figure of 12 million for 1991, some 20 per cent of the population.

The rural exodus began in the early 1960s due to a combination mechanisation and demographic growth. It underwent a marked acceleration in the 1970s and 80s. In 1965, 72.2 per cent of the inhabitants of Kurdistan were rural as against 61.5 per cent in 1980 and perhaps 55 per cent in 1991.

Part of the exodus is towards the regional capitals of Diyarbakir, Van, Bitlis and Siirt which have seen a great deal of development. Nonetheless, the poor industrial capacities of these towns condemn the majority of Kurds to an economic migration towards the great agglomerations of western Turkey. Istanbul has thus become the premier Kurdish town, with an estimated immigrant population of approximately 800,000. A third of all Kurds born in Kurdistan today live in a strictly Turkish speaking region of Turkey.

In consequence and for the first time since the 1940s, the rate of demographic growth has become negative in the Kurdish provinces of Tunceli, Kars, and Erzincan, zero in Urfa and, generally, less than the average for the whole of Turkey (20.65 in the other Kurdish regions). This trend will probably continue, even if the dam planned for the Euphrates (GAP), which will be completed before the end of the decade, can reverse the trend at least for the environs of Urfa.

In Turkey, there are Kurds in eighteen provinces: Adiyaman, Agri, Bingöl, Bitlis, Diyarbakir, Elazig, Erzincan, Erzurum, Gazi, Hakkari, Kars, Malatya, Mardin, Mus, Siirt, Tunceli, Urfa and Van. Furthermore, there are Kurdish district attached to Turkish provinces; in Hatay, Maras and Sivas around a third of the population is Kurdish. There have been important Kurdish communities (Haymana, Kulu, Cihanbeyli, Ankara) living in central Anatolia since the Ottoman or Kemalist era. Conversely, the population of the provinces in the east is not entirely Kurdish. Turks, Azeris and Arabs make up possibly 20 per cent of the population in these areas.

The economy

Until the 1960s, the economy of the Kurdish regions was largely self-sufficient based on animal husbandry and non mechanised agriculture. Economic links were traditionally with Syria or Iraq, particularly through smuggling. Integration was delayed by the poor lines of communication. Apart from its military investments the Turkish state effected a non-interventionist policy, although everywhere else the state takes initiatives and shows itself to be in favour of a planned economy. The number of doctors in the Kurdish zones is four times fewer than the other Turkish regions. The local medical personnel, often poorly motivated, would prefer to relocate to another area rather than remain in a region without any infrastructures or any city life. The banking network is underdeveloped; loans are often made by individuals at exorbitant rates, which slows down investment. Because of the insecurity, Turkish industrialists will not invest in the east where the infrastructure is archaic. The local bourgeoisie often prefers to invest in the west of Turkey where the possibilities are greater. Today, less than 10 per cent of the population of the east works in industry and the 18 provinces with Kurdish majorities contribute 3 per cent to the industrial output of the country (six provinces have a level of industrialisation which is statistically zero). Moreover, the industries are often brick-works with little effect on training. In fact the beginnings of industrialisation are built on the mining industries: phosphate, chromium (at Maden), iron (at Divrigi) and oil, all of which are state controlled.

Only the South-East Development Project, through the construction of a dam on the Euphrates, will bring the start of industrialisation to a conclusion and with it a net change in the way of life of the local peasant population. This project, with its first phase due to be completed in 1993, involves 21 dams and 17 hydro-electric stations on the Euphrates and the Tigris.

Besides the rural exodus, the consequence is that the population is becoming urbanised but not industrialised, while the protest movements are spreading more and more away from their urban starting points.

As far as agriculture is concerned, the first free elections held in 1950, marked the beginning of the economic integration of the Kurdish regions, with the development of the cultivation of sugar beet, cotton and tobacco for both local markets and export. In the case of tobacco, the Turkish government forced the Kurdish growers to surrender their crops at fixed prices to the National Tobacco Agency. The growers of the Black Sea and the Aegean were not treated in this way.

Agriculture started to become mechanised with the introduction of agricultural machinery in far fewer quantities than the national average. Land distribution was extremely unequal: one-sixth of the proprietors owned three-quarters of the cultivable land. This favoured the modernisation of fairly vast properties, but forced the small owners who were unable to adapt into exodus. In general, the great properties grew up on the basis of the expropriation of communal lands or *waqf* (holdings managed by religious groups) aided by the adoption of the Swiss civil code and to the benefit of the tribal chiefs.

With the transformation of tribal social structures, many of the traditional leaders (aghas, *shaikhs*) became city dwellers. As this happened, so their power over the populations would tend to weaken and, sometimes, the taxes that they had received would then go to nationalist organisations.

In recent years, the investment situation has worsened for two main reasons. First of all, since 1987, it has been apparent that the state, pursuing policies of denationalisation, etc., has been anxious to distance itself from the economic policy which had been traditionally interventionist since Kemal Atatürk. Secondly, the assassinations, acts of sabotage, and other activities of the PKK posed a supplementary risk for private investments which underwent a marked decline.

According to a survey by the Istanbul Chamber of Industry, fourteen of the eighteen Kurdish provinces occupy the bottom of the list for the distribution of gross national income for the period of 1979 to 1986. In these areas, the average income is less than one-fifteenth of that of a resident of Istanbul or Izmir. There are only two exceptions: the province of Elazig where the principle chromium deposit is situated, and Malatya because of its agricultural and commercial dynamism. The province at the bottom of the list is Hakkari, near the Iraqi and Iranian borders, with an income of less than 100 dollars a year.

Education and culture

The basic school system suffers from a severe shortage of materials and personnel. In 1980 only 33 per cent of all those over six years old had been educated, the figure for women reaching 19 per cent. The backwardness is considerable in comparison to Turkey as a whole, where almost 60 per cent of the population have attended school. Today, there are only about ten establishments of higher education in the whole region.

Since Kurdish was banned in 1924, Kurdish intellectuals like the novelist Yashar Kemal or the film-maker Yilmaz Güney, have expressed themselves in Turkish. Meanwhile an estimated two-thirds of the Kurds from the eastern provinces speak Turkish badly.

From the 1950s onwards the speaking of the language began to be tolerated, but publications and the importing of Kurdish works (decree of 25th January 1967) remained banned. In practice, the situation has evolved over the past few years towards a tolerance, never made official, of the occasional publication in the Kurdish language.

It has been government policy to aim to turkise the names of Kurdish towns and villages. Just as 'Eastern Anatolia' or the provinces of the east are used instead of the geographic term 'Kurdistan', there have been many attempts to change the names of towns or villages. Dersim, for example, is now called 'Tunceli'. One of the first decrees of the Committee for National Union which arose out of the military *coup d'état* of 17th May 1960 was concerned with the names of Kurdish towns and villages.

Kurdish music, which is much respected and which used to be scholarly, has become distinctly impoverished over the past few decades due mainly to the banning of the traditional music schools.

The Kurdish traditional costume (shirt and voluminous trousers) was banned during the most extreme periods of repression. It is, at present, tolerated by the authorities.

The destruction of Kurdish monuments, essential to the identity of a community, has been systematically effected. Buildings erected at the time of the Kurdish principalities have been a particular target. The Birca Belek (Palace of Many Colours), built by the Bedirkhans at Jezira Botan on the banks of the Tigris, was razed to the ground. Similarly, in the past few years, Armenian churches have been destroyed in eastern Anatolia.

The *mullahs* played an important role in the cultural and social life of a village. They were dependent on the population for their subsistence and, apart from the basics of the religion, they taught the children the rudiments of poetry or Kurdish literature. In 1963 the government instituted the system which organised the *mullahs* along the lines of the civil service. The *mullahs*, who were from then on educated in government schools, lost their local legitimacy and were sometimes even accused of being government agents. They no longer played, as once they did, the role of guardians of Kurdish tradition.

Nonetheless, the Turkish government has made a recent step towards the recognition of Kurdish culture, by proposing, on 27th January 1991, to repeal the 1983 law which banned the use of Kurdish in public. On that occasion, Mr Ozal had even stated explicitly to a journalist that one in six people in Turkey were Kurdish. The fact that this proposition did not encounter any serious opposition is a sign of the times. Even General Kenan Evren, despite having being one of the principal players in the 1980 *coup d'état*, declared himself in favour of the proposition. The only open opposition came from the extreme right wing party led by M. Turkes .

The way for this governmental evolution had been prepared by an evolution of the political parties such as the SHP (Social Democratic Populist Party). On 9th May 1990, Inönü, the leader of the SHP, called for the creation of a Kurdish Institute within the framework of Turkey's universities. This declaration, which was made in Van, could be explained by a sharp decline in the party's popularity and the desire to recuperate a far from marginal electorate.

For all that, schooling in Turkish, the Turkish speaking environment and a Kurdish language cut off from the oral tradition of its elders contributed to a rapid acculturation. Quite quickly, Kurdish culture has become residual and, if one can still dance to traditional Kurdish tunes, the words are in Turkish. It is clear that the danger for Kurdish culture, isolated from any contemporary evolution, is that it may become folkloric and proceed little by little into the field of ethnographic curiosity.

Kurdish political life

The integration of the Kurds into the Turkish political process

The liberalisation of the Turkish political regime began after the war. The economic difficulties and the famines of the years 1940 to 45 resulted in a general movement of dissatisfaction which induced Ismet Inonü to change the regime. In 1946, several parties were created. One of these was the Democratic Party which went on to a convincing win in the 1950 elections. Founded by the wealthy landowner Adnan Menderes and Celal Bayar, who had served as a prime minister under Mustafa Kemal Atatürk, the Democratic Party was not carrying any plans for a break with Kemalism.

Its arrival in power in 1950 nevertheless heralded a period of democratisation which particularly benefited the Kurds who had voted for the party *en masse*. Police repression was substantially reduced and a number of exiles were allowed to return to Kurdistan where they were able to regain possession of their land (these were often tribal chiefs). The Democratic Party, which initiated a few projects to improve amenities (hospitals and roads), managed to politically integrate the Kurdish leaders, many of whom became parliamentary deputies and even ministers.

The Kemalist reaction came from the army, which found its own political marginalisation hard to tolerate, and which saw the country's economic difficulties as a justification for its return to the fray. Following the military *coup d'état* of 27th May 1960, Menderes declared that the Kurds had attempted, by using their political positions within the Democratic Party, to obtain the independence of Kurdistan. In June 1960, the authorities had 485 Kurdish notables arrested and detained for several months; 55 of the most influential were exiled to the west of the country for two years. Almost all of them were members of Menderes's Democratic Party.

In May 1961 there were demonstrations in the principal Kurdish towns, particularly Diyarbakir, Bitlis and Van, in response to the military policy of a return to Kemalist orthodoxy. The demonstrators carried banners demanding the recognition of Kurdish identity. These gatherings symbolised the renaissance of a Kurdish movement which had been decapitated before the war.

The new constitution of 1961, which marked the return to power of a civilian administration, did not lift the ban on 'regionalist' parties, but the opening up of the political process was to give the Kurds indirect means of expression.

In the second half of February 1961, three new parties were born: the Justice Party (JP), the New Turkey Party (NTP) and the Turkish Workers' Party (TWP).

No clear majority emerged from the 1961 election, but the Justice Party came in first. The Justice Party and the New Turkey Party shared the votes of the electors from the East. One of the leaders of the latter, Doctor Yusuf Azizoglu, was a Kurd who became Minister of Health in June 1962 under the presidency of Ismet Inönü.

Because of Azizoglu's extremely dynamic policy of building hospitals and dispensaries in the East, Bekata, the Minister of the Interior who was close to Ismet Inönü, accused him of 'regionalism'. This led to his resignation.

The fact that the Kurds were prohibited from forming a party with regionalist foundations along with their natural opposition to Kemalist ideology explains why so many of them joined left wing organisations. Sometimes, their presence became preponderant. This happened in the Turkish Workers' Party (TWP), a Marxist organisation whose second president, Mehmet Ali Aslan, was a Kurdish lawyer from the Ararat region. In 1966 he published the first Kurdish socialist review, which was banned after its fourth edition and which led to his internment. Within the TWP at that time, the Kurdish question was theoretically 'resolved' by Marxist dogmas: the alliance of the 'working classes' and the establishment of a 'socialist regime'. The TWP set up branches in Kurdistan during the 1960s and, in the end, it was the Kurdish question that finished off the TWP which was already consumed by internal conflicts. During the course of its congress in October 1970, a resolution was adopted which recognised the 'Kurdish people'. It was the first time that a party that was represented in the National Assembly (15 seats out of 450 in the 1965 election) took such a position.

Nihat Erim's government reacted by banning the TWP for 'pro-Kurdish separatist activities'. Its principal ruling members were arrested and sentenced to up to twelve years in prison. They were set free by the July 1974 amnesty which was introduced by the government that came to power following the October 1973 election.

The rise of the Kurdish nationalist parties

After the *coup d'état* in 1971, a number of militant Kurds in the TWP established a clandestine political group called the Socialist Party of Turkish Kurdistan (SPTK). Because its aims made the party illegal it chose a bilingual review *Riyâ Azâdi* (The Way of Liberty) as a legal front. Youth organisations were set up from 1976. These were known as the Revolutionary Cultural Associations of the People, and very soon there were over twenty of these organisations in Kurdistan and in Anatolia. In

1977, the publication of a Kurdo-Turkish newspaper, *Roja Wela* (Sun of the Fatherland), was interrupted after a few months by the establishment of martial law which also suppressed the youth organisations. The 1980 *coup d'état* brought an end to the clandestine existence of the SPTK. A number of its leaders were arrested, its Secretary General, Kemal Burkay, managed to leave Turkey and took over the publication of *Riyâ Azâdi* from abroad.

The SPTK had a Marxist, pro-Soviet programme. Its strategy was to rally all the 'anti-imperialist' forces within a united front for the whole of Turkey. It was more a Marxist than a nationalist movement, and advocated the federation of two socialist states (Turkish and Kurdish) in Turkey. Armed struggle was not on its agenda and its effect was primarily ideological.

At the beginning of the 1980s, the SPTK signed an agreement with two other movements on a Marxist inspired platform: the Democratic and Cultural Revolutionary Association and the Partisans of the National Liberation of Kurdistan.

The KDPT (Kurdistan Democratic Party of Turkey) was created in 1965, in the image of the KDP-Iraq, by Faik Bucak, a lawyer and the parliamentary deputy for Urfa. In 1969, when the faction close to Barzani was in control of the party, there was a split. Doctor Siwan created a party with the same name, but which, in 1977, was to become the Workers' Party of Kurdistan then, in 1983, the vanguard of the Workers of Kurdistan. The creation of the SPTK further weakened the KDP. The last split took place in 1979 with the birth of the KUK (Partisans of the National Liberation of Kurdistan). Today, what remains of the KDPT is only a nucleus of the Barzani faithful. It remains conservative, even though since the congress of October 1977 there appeared to be a rapprochement with the Marxists. Its programme is distinctly for the independence of Kurdistan and not for autonomy, although in practice this can be less clear cut.

The vanguard of the Workers of Kurdistan gained official recognition in 1983 after a congress in the Near-East, but its origins go back a long way. It was a clandestine party from the moment it was created (it had its first congress in 1975). The SPTK's plan was that organisations with a good following of women and young people should operate as legal intermediaries for the party. In Turkey, the Womens' Democratic and Revolutionary Cultural Associations were better known than the party itself. In 1982, a serious internal crisis led to a split from which the party, already weakened by the arrests that followed the 1980 *coup d'état*, would never really recover. The party, which drew a great deal of its support from teachers and students, maintained a Marxist pro-Soviet bias.

The Partisans of the National Liberation of Kurdistan was founded in 1979-80 following a split in the KDPT. It was pro-independence and was one of the only non-Marxist movements. A large number of its members were young people who had lost their social standing, and there were many in such a position in a society in the throes of transformation.

There was also a significant number of small groups: *Rizgâri* (Liberation), Marxist and pro-independence; *Ala Rizgâri* (the Flag of Liberty), a split from the former; *Kawa* (maoist); and *Têkosin* (the Struggle).

Finally, in 1988, an Islamic Party of Kurdistan appeared, which was in favour of a unified and Islamic Kurdish state. It recruited its members from amongst the intellectuals, the members of the *Sufi Naqshbandi* brotherhood and the former supporters of the authorised religious parties. It was critical of the Iranian Revolution and seemed closer to Saudi Arabia from which it received financial support. The appearance of a party claiming itself to be Islamic was something new in Kurdistan which had been, almost exclusively, the territory of the Marxist parties. Nevertheless, it was only partly surprising. Islamic ideology is today the only alternative to the nationalist Kemalist model which dominates Turkish political life.

The PKK

The PKK (Workers' Party of Kurdistan) is currently the most successfully established party in Kurdistan and warrants a more detailed analysis.

Its ancestry can be traced back to a student meeting at the University of Ankara. From that moment, Abdullah Ocalan, who was a student at Ankara's Faculty of Political Sciences, asserted himself as the leader of the movement. Abdullah Ocalan's nickname is 'Apo' (uncle).

The group's strategy was to distance itself from the other movements which were perceived as too involved with the government. It began its first propaganda activities in 1975. Abdullah Ocalan operated in his native town of Urfa while other activist went to Dersim. At that time, the group's activities consisted mainly of secret meetings with students and other young people. From the outset, the tone of their propaganda was nationalist and violent. Texts such as *The Way of the Kurdish Revolution*, distributed in 1975, contained extremely brutal attacks on the Kurdish bourgeoisie, accused of collaboration with the Turkish state. The party is Marxist and the Soviet Union, without being a model, is regarded with respect. Its programme was simple and radical. The independence of Kurdistan as the prerequisite for the construction of an authentically communist society through the elimination of the middle class and the taking of power by an alliance of workers and peasants. In 1977 there was a split in the group. The organisation based in Gaziantep quarrelled with Abdullah Ocalan who ordered the execution of its leaders, Ali Yaylacik and Mehmet Uzun. Generally speaking, most of the violence during this embryonic period was aimed at those who collaborated with the regime in Kurdistan or at the other parties rather than directly at the Turkish state.

The PKK was officially formed on 27th November 1978 near Diyarbakir. Ocalan was appointed General Secretary at the head of a central committee of seven people (only one of whom had been present at the founding meeting in 1974). In order to focus some attention on the creation of the PKK a plan to assassinate Mehmet Celal Bucak was devised. Bucak was an important landowner in the Siverek area, the archetypal 'collaborator' and leader of pro-government militias. Bucak survived the murder attempt and his militias began an offensive against the PKK. At the same time, as part of its all round offensive strategy to become the dominant party, the PKK launched its troops against the Partisans of the National Liberation of Kurdistan which was well established locally. It was the beginning of a war between the two parties which was to produce numerous victims. At the time, the PKK was a party which appeared to be essentially against the propertied classes, which supported social struggle and the elimination of competing parties rather than action against the Turkish state.

At the time of the 1980 *coup d'état*, the PKK was principally established in three areas: 1) Gaziantep, Kahramanmaras and Malatya; 2) Urfa, Diyarbakir and Mardin; 3) Elazig, Tunceli and Bingöl. In the mounting anarchy of the end of the 1970s, the PKK financed itself through bank raids and dealing in arms and drugs.

Abdullah Ocalan probably anticipated the 1980 *coup d'état*. He fled to Syria where he remains to this day. Most of the PKK's leaders joined him after the *coup d'état*. The PKK held its first congress at the Syria-Lebanon frontier. One of the delegates put Ocalan in a difficult position. Ocalan had him executed shortly afterwards and re-emerged as the uncontested leader at the second congress in 1982. During this congress, the PKK adopted a strategy of selective terrorism against the Turkish state and its Kurdish collaborators.

In May 1983, three Turkish army soldiers were killed in a PKK ambush. The army reacted by launching a major search operation on Iraqi territory with the authorisation of the Baghdad government. A short time later, an alliance was drawn up between the PKK and Masoud Barzani's Iraqi KDP. Barzani had been on the lookout for a new ally since the decline of the Partisans of the National Liberation of Kurdistan which had been his main ally up until then. This alliance would allow PKK activists who, until then, had been trained in Syria or the Bekaa plain, also to become established in the north of Iraq.

At the beginning, the PKK, whenever possible, travelled about with doctors, as a measure calculated to attract the sympathy of the population, and modelled its organisation on the Vietcong. Abbas Kalkan (arrested in Germany in 1989 after his split with Ocalan) was, at that time, head of the several hundred strong military forces of the PKK. PKK attacks continued throughout 1984, but fell off during the course of 1985. Then, in August

1986, there was a particularly murderous operation in which twelve gendarmes from the Hakkari district were killed. In retaliation, the Turkish army shelled PKK camps in Iraq causing 150 casualties (some of these belonged to Barzani's KDP-Iraq). Barzani, probably disturbed by the Turkish reactions, began to distance himself from Ocalan.

It was during this period that the PKK launched a series of actions against Kurdish collaborators. The violence of these actions alienated the sympathy of the population from the PKK and provoked the opposition of other Kurdish political forces. On 20th June 1987, during a PKK attack on the village of Pinarcik (in the province of Mardin) which had been accused of collaboration, 30 people (including 16 children and 8 women) were killed.

The successes of the guerilla war during 1987 were compromised by the end of the alliance with Barzani's KDP-Iraq, which now considered it dangerous to support a party involved in terrorist actions against civilians and which was becoming a threat to the KDP-Iraq itself.

In addition, the PKK's relations with the other Kurdish parties were at their lowest. There had been armed clashes with several of them. The PKK's appeal for unity amongst the Kurdish parties only succeeded in precipitating the institution of an anti-PKK front. On 23rd June 1988, eight organisations came together to form a common front called *Tegver* ('The Movement' in Kurdish). *Tegver,* whose leader was Kemal Bukay was a pro-independence movement, but opposed to terrorism. More seriously for the PKK, a split occurred within the movement: Hussein Yildirim, a lawyer living in Sweden, founded the Kurdish Workers' Revolutionary Party.

With the aid of reformed members of the group, the Turkish police successfully dismantled a part of the PKK's infrastructure: in 1989 two of its regional leaders, Halit Celik from the region of Garzan and Mehmet Emin Karatay of Mardin, were arrested. Faced with this series of setbacks, the PKK's strategy evolved appreciably. Actions against civilians were abandoned in favour of economic targets. The first application of this new policy was the attack on the Siirt coal mine in May 1989. A PKK commando unit occupied the mine and, taking advantage of animosity between the villagers and the management of the works, organised a propaganda meeting which concluded with the enrolment (or removal) of a score of young people.

The PKK was also seeking new alliances. The rapprochement with Talabani's PUK, which began in 1988, was a compensation for the loss of support from Barzani's PDKI. The PKK also started to co-operate with small leftist groups such as *Dev Sol* (Revolutionary Left) and the Turkish Marxist-Leninist Communist Party. This provided the PKK with logistic support in the towns.

In 1990 there was an outbreak of incidents in the urban areas: children and adolescents threw stones at soldiers; on 23rd March 1990, thousands of people demonstrated and chanted slogans in Mardin. The PKK had succeeded in finding a social support base in the urban areas and, after the massive rejection of its attacks on civilians, appeared to be enjoying a certain popularity. The seven or so years of guerilla warfare had produced thousands of victims, as many of them amongst the civilian population as amongst the military and the members of the PKK. There has been no reduction in the intensity of these actions. On the contrary, their incidence has increased during the course of the years. Since 1983, the Turkish army has crossed into Iraqi territory on mopping-up operations on numerous occasions. During the course of the summer and autumn of 1991, the Turkish armed forces undertook several raids while a series of arrests took place amongst the Kurds of Turkey.

3. The Kurds of Iraq

The formation of the Iraqi state and Shaikh Mahmud's revolt

Iraq was a British creation. The break-up of the Ottoman Empire during the First World War allowed the British Empire to take control of the *vilayets* (provinces) of Basra and Baghdad, that is to say southern Mesopotamia. The inclusion of the *vilayet* of Mosul, with its Kurdish majority population, was linked to the presence of oil in this province.

It wasn't until the armistice of Mudros on 30th October 1918 that the British occupied the *vilayet* of Mosul. In fact, it was only a partial occupation because of the Kurdish nationalist movement led by Shaikh Mahmud Barzinji which held the Sulaymaniya region. This movement, which was put down by the British army, expressed the refusal of the Kurds to being dominated again by Turkey or to be included in an Arab state.

In order to form the Iraqi state, the British called upon Emir Faisal who had been driven out of Damascus in July 1920. Meanwhile, the Treaty of Sèvres of 10th August allowed General Sharif Pasha, who had been a Kurdish officer in the Ottoman army and the Turkish Ambassador to Stockholm, to give a voice to Kurdish demands. The treaty in fact anticipated the eventual constitution of a Kurdish state consisting of the Kurdish regions included in the Ottoman Empire. Article 64 of the treaty even called for the 'voluntary' union of the inhabitants of the *vilayet* of Mosul.

This last provision would oblige the British, who had put their plan for the creation of Iraq before the Cairo Conference in March 1921, to arrange a referendum in the *vilayet* of Mosul. In May 1921a vote was organised to determine the opinion of the population concerned. The vote, its franchise based on property ownership, had an extremely poor poll and British pressure turned it into a simple pretext for annexation. A second ballot, equally manipulated, allowed the election of King Faisal. Once Faisal was in power, he needed to affirm his authority over his new kingdom. All the more so since he was a *Sunni* and his subjects, the majority being *Shi'ite*, did not take well to him. Faisal began to push for the effective control of the *vilayet* of Mosul which until then had been under British rule. At that time, the Iraqi-Kurdish frontier had still not been defined.

The coming to power of the Kemalists in 1922 led to the reopening of the Mosul question by Turkey, which wanted to regain control of the *vilayet*. In fact, the Kemalists had already initiated a campaign of unrest as early as June 1921. This was very quickly successful. A year later the uprisings multiplied under the guidance of a Turkish officer Ali Shafik ('Oz

Demir'), forcing the British troops out of Sulaymaniya in September. In order to check the Turkish advance, the British used Shaikh Mahmud, the only leader who had sufficient influence to bring the troubles to an end and thereby to avoid the costs of a military reconquest. On his return to Sulaymaniya in October 1922, Shaikh Mahmud announced the formation of a cabinet and, on the 18th November, proclaimed himself 'King of Kurdistan'. Rapidly, an embryonic administration was formed and a newspaper *Roj-e-Kurdistan* published.

Relations with the British deteriorated following the appearance of two areas of friction. First, the status of Kirkuk, which Shaikh Mahmud wanted to administer against the wishes of the British who had linked it up with Baghdad. Then, far from launching any operations against the Turks, as the British had hoped, Shaikh Mahmud attempted to play the two powers off against each other in order to strengthen his own position.

But the British were, for the time being, standing by their joint declaration with Iraq of 22nd December 1922 in which they recognised the right of the Kurdish people to form a government within the borders of Iraq.

The failure of the first Lausanne conference in February 1923, led the British government to change its policy. The British accused Shaikh Mahmud of indulging in partisan unrest and of having contacts with the *Shi'ite* rebels in the South. RAF planes dropped leaflets over Sulaymaniya calling for Shaikh Mahmud's surrender. He withdrew from the town on 4th March 1923 and took refuge in the mountains with some of his followers to continue the struggle. The British forces then launched an offensive to prevent Shaikh Mahmud joining forces with the Turks, who retreated from Rawandiz without a fight. After that, the nationalist leader was forced to flee to Persia.

The British military victory, as complete as it was, was difficult to exploit politically because of the Kurdish leaders' opposition to Faisal and the influence that Shaikh Mahmud retained, despite his exile. The British therefore left Sulaymaniya in June 1923. But, in anticipation of Shaikh Mahmud's return, they attached several Kurdish districts to Arab regions, thereby rendering meaningless their autonomous status. Shaikh Mahmud's attempts to regain a foothold in the Kurdish districts led the RAF to resume bombing raids in December 1923.

The last episode of Kurdish resistance was the unrest in the *vilayet* after the legislative elections of March 1924, followed by fresh bombing raids by the RAF. This brought about the British occupation of Sulaymaniya in July 1924.

After the Treaty of Lausanne, signed in July 1923, the council of the League of Nations sent an international commission of enquiry to the *vilayet* of Mosul. The commission stayed there from January to March 1925 and established undeniably the existence of a Kurdish language and a Kurdish identity. In the end, on 16th December 1925, the council of the League of Nations decided in favour of the attachment of Mosul to Iraq and fixed the frontier between Iraq and Turkey. As the mandated power, the British government was invited to report to the League of Nations on the conditions of administration of the *vilayet* of Mosul, to promulgate within it a form of autonomy, and to give recognition to the rights of the Kurds. The only concrete application was Baghdad's promulgation in 1926 of the Local Languages Law, which allowed the Kurds (in Sulaymaniya and Arbil) to have a primary education in their own language and to print books in Kurdish.

Meanwhile, although Shaikh Mahmud had taken refuge on the Iraqi-Iranian border, he was not out of the political picture. Already, in 1925, the Iraqi government had launched a campaign against deserters who had sought refuge with friendly tribes in Iran. The following year, in 1926, a similar operation was attempted with the collaboration of an Iranian column which suffered a painful defeat. Once again, RAF attacks forced Shaikh Mahmud to negotiate with a British emissary, Mr Cornwallis, during the autumn of 1926. However, they were finally unable to reach any agreement.

At that time, the whole of Iraqi Kurdistan was refusing to accept an Arab administration, despite Baghdad's promises regarding the use of Kurdish as an official language. Various Kurdish cultural societies were formed between 1926 and 1927, with a success which was to contribute to their taking an increasingly political stance. For some time, Mosul became the hub of the nationalist movement, until the intervention of police operations, conducted by the British, dismantled the clandestine organisations. Despite the resolution of the council of the League of Nations in 1925, which settled the problem in international law, Baghdad's control over Kurdistan was still not in fact assured at the time of Iraq's accession to independence in June 1930. The Anglo-Iraqi treaty, which ended the colonial government's mandate, made no mention of the rights of the Kurds. In response, petitions were sent by the notables of Sulaymaniya reminding of the December 1925 decision of the council of the League of Nations. Tension mounted and, on 6th September 1930, troops shot into a crowd at Sulaymaniya killing dozens of people. The Iraqi government then took advantage of the troubles to initiate an upsurge of arrests amongst the Kurdish nationalists. Shaikh Mahmud then decided to put pressure on the League of Nations by organising petition campaigns. Alongside this diplomatic effort, he attempted, without success, to take the village of Panjwin, but his troops were beaten off.

The repression did not begin until after the League of Nations had rejected the Kurdish demands. In April 1931, Shaikh Mahmud's troops suffered a severe defeat and he crossed over into Iran. Thereafter, he was forced to give himself up to the Baghdad government, which kept him under house arrest until his death in 1956.

The first Barzani rebellion (1943-45)

The family of the *shaikhs* of Barzan has played a central role in the Kurdish nationalist movement since the 1930s up until the present day. The first revolt to win them fame was in the Ottoman era and led to the arrest and then the hanging of its leader, Shaikh Abdel Salam.

His brother Shaikh Ahmed was at the heart of a movement of revolt which only ended in 1934, with the exile of the whole family. In 1927, Shaikh Ahmed wanted to extend his zone of influence, and came up against British forces who were building a fort a few kilometres from Barzan. This was at a time when Shaikh Ahmed wielded considerable religious authority.

The real rebellion began in 1931, when Shaikh Ahmed sent several hundred men to support the Kurdish revolt of Mount Ararat, by then in disarray. This act of solidarity was not at all appreciated by the Turkish authorities, who urged Baghdad to intervene. The Iraqi government intervened indirectly by supporting his neighbour, Shaikh Rashid. After Shaikh Rashid's defeat, the government in Baghdad launched a series of military operations in 1931-32 which, with the ever-effective support of the RAF, led to the crushing of the revolt and Shaikh Ahmed's exile to Sulaymaniya. Nevertheless, two of his brothers continued the guerilla struggle which was to keep the whole region in a state of insecurity until 1934.

In parallel with these movements, a party called *Hewa* (Hope) emerged in 1941. It was the result of the fusion of two organisations which had, until then, shared the support of the nationalists. On the one side, *Brayati* (Brotherhood), a group which had been established along the lines of the Kurdish clubs of Constantinople, which brought together notables and intellectuals and which was dominated by Shaikh Latif, one of the sons of Shaikh Ahmed. On the other, *Karker*, an association of young progressists close to the Iraqi CP. The fusion of these two organisations did not stop political leanings from being maintained, particularly those on the Marxist left. The new party was based in Baghdad and developed branches in the principal towns of Kurdistan.

Hewa was in fact to be the organisational base of the new leader, a member of the Barzani family, Mullah Mustafa Barzani. After he was sentenced, along with Shaikh Ahmed, to house arrest in Sulaymaniya, Mullah Mustafa Barzani found himself, for want of government aid, in financial difficulties. These difficulties certainly strengthened his determination to escape and, in 1943, he managed to leave Sulaymaniya and return to his fief, Barzan. The fugitive's attempts to open diplomatic channels to Baghdad were not successful and the number of incidents increased dramatically.

In December 1943, Barzani, who had beaten off every attack by the Iraqi army, was hoping for British intervention in his favour. The British did, in fact, put pressure on the strong man of Baghdad, Nuri Saïd. Saïd was aware of the weakness of the central government's position and agreed to negotiations. These brought tangible results: a general amnesty for the rebels and the withdrawal of the army. In February 1944, Barzani went to Baghdad at the head of a delegation of Kurdish chieftains. But the situation deteriorated for want of a satisfactory compromise between the Kurdish leader and the Iraqi authorities. Moreover, as the end of the war approached, the British ceased playing intermediary between Baghdad and the Kurds, which further increased the impossibility of any negotiated settlement being reached.

The fighting started again during the summer of 1945, sparked off by Baghdad's decision to reopen police stations in Sulaymaniya, exacerbated by the British refusal to intervene directly from then on. Betrayed by rival chiefs, particularly his father in law Mahmud Agha Zibari, Barzani and his followers were forced to seek refuge in Iran, where he directed the armed forces in the ephemeral Mahabad republic. After it came to grief, Barzani spent eleven years in exile in the USSR.

Barzani's defeat, immediately caused by the tribal structure of the society, could also be explained by his relations with the *Hewa* party. While the party, under the influence of its left wing, maintained a pro-Soviet and 'anti-imperialist' (meaning 'anti-British') line, Barzani was counting on good relations with the British in the hope of obtaining the international recognition which the Kurds so desperately lacked.

Barzani's fall split the *Hewa* party into different factions, some of which were close to the Iraqi CP while others were more conservative. However, under the Mahabad republic, Mustafa Barzani created the Kurdistan Democratic Party of Iraq (KDP-Iraq) along the lines of the Iranian KDP. In August 1946, the KDP-Iraq held its first congress in secret in Baghdad. The structure (with a central committee, and politburo) and programme of the party were directly inspired by the young progressive intellectuals of the movement.

Deprived of a leader because of Barzani's exile, the party was severely affected by a wave of police repression which led to the arrest of its general staff in January 1947. At that moment, what remained of the KDPI was in effect controlled by the Iraqi CP. Under the influence of the latter, the KDPI became overtly Marxist and gave precedence to the anti-imperialist struggle rather than the national. In doing so it was adopting the arguments of the Iraqi CP which was in favour of self-determination for Kurdistan, while at the same time stigmatising separatist ideas.

The end of the monarchy and the 1961 war

General Qasim seized power on 14th July 1958. This awakened fresh hope in the Kurds, since the provisional constitution of 7th July recognised, for the first time, that the Arabs and the Kurds were associates in Iraq. The constitution guaranteed their respective national rights within the Iraqi entity. Symbolically, the arms of the new republic were made up of an Arab sword crossed with a Kurdish dagger. However, article 2 proclaimed that 'The state of Iraq is a part of the Arab Nation', and the Kurdish minority felt uneasy about Aref, who championed union with Syria and Egypt. Finally Qasim asserted himself over Aref, with the support of the Kurds and the Iraqi CP which followed the line that had been laid down in Moscow.

After the downfall of the monarchy, Barzani returned to Iraq. During a visit to Cairo he met Nasser. Given a hero's welcome, Barzani returned to Barzan where he met his brother Shaikh Ahmed. General Barzani was at that time playing a pro-Soviet game in close concert with the Iraqi CP. It was thus that the pro-Aref uprising in Mosul, in March 1959, was defeated in part by the Kurdish militias who 'cleaned up' the suburbs of the town, leaving several hundred people dead. From that moment on, the alliance between Qasim, the KDPI and the Iraqi CP was sealed, at the price of an alignment, which was to become ever more total, between the KDPI and the Iraqi CP.

Barzani underwent a sudden about-face in May 1959, during the revolt of the Kurdish leaders of Rawandiz who had been frightened by agrarian reform and the arrival of communist militias. The uprising was quickly brought under control but 20,000 people sought refuge in Iran. It was on this occasion that Barzani became aware of the Iraqi CP's growing stranglehold on the KDPI. He decided to take the KDPI in hand again and accused the Iraqi CP of having attempted to have him assassinated. He wanted to force out the pro-communists in favour of a new team of young intellectuals, Ibrahim Ahmad, and his future son-in-law Jalal Talabani. This eviction of the communists was a sign of what was to come a few months later when, in January 1960, Qasim outlawed the Iraqi CP (while authorising one of its dissident groups). The KDPI remained a legal party, but there was increasing tension between Barzani and Qasim, who wanted the suppression of the reference in the party's programme to the autonomy of Kurdistan. This was turned down by the congress of the KDPI. In his anxiety to achieve a calculated delay, General Barzani allowed representatives of the Iranian KDP to be thrown out of Iraq and looked for support from Moscow, where he spent two months at the end of 1961 and the beginning of 1962, and was able to discuss matters with Kruschev.

But the breakdown in relations with Qasim was inescapable. Kurdish language newspapers were banned, KDPI leaders were arrested and General Barzani sought refuge in Barzan. Qasim, who had adopted an increasingly nationalist attitude (notably with respect to claims over Kuwait), was to unleash the war which, despite some truces, still endures today. The history of Iraqi Kurdistan has repeated itself ceaselessly throughout these years: succeeding governments in Baghdad have made concessions to Kurdish nationalists at times of weakness of the central state. Then, as soon as circumstances permit, and because they have been unable to accept a Kurdish autonomy which, as they see it, may at any moment erupt into independence, they take up the offensive once more. This is the background for the series of signed but never respected agreements, which have only confirmed that it is impossible for Baghdad to defeat the Kurds by military means, and which therefore amount to no more than truces.

In Kurdistan, clashes began to occur between two traditionally rival tribes: the Barzanis and the Zibaris. The latter were beaten, but there followed a wave of unrest in Kurdistan which was used by the government in Baghdad as a pretext for sending in the army in September 1961. The KDPI's wish to see Barzani marginalised, along with the Iraqi CP's attitude (it refused to take up arms), led the KDPI to wait until March 1962 before joining Barzani in the struggle. This was also the date when the Iraqi CP changed its attitude. This absence of the KDPI, and consequently of any organised militant infrastructure, explains the defeats that the Kurds underwent during the first year. General Barzani and several hundred of his men abandoned Barzan to take refuge in the Zakho mountains, sheltering from the Iraqi forces.

The insurgents's side was considerably strengthened when the KDPI entered the struggle, but the movement remained divided: Barzani controlled the north of Kurdistan, the KDPI controlled the south. In addition, whilst Barzani was still theoretically the president of the KDPI, he refused to have any relations with the party. Jalal Talabani and Ibrahim Ahmed took over as leaders of the KDPI and, as intellectuals, opposed Barzani's 'tribal' authority. Barzani's stature asserted itself in the struggle. He became the symbol of the Kurdish resistance and the KDPI recognised him, *nolens volens*, as the movement's principal figure.

Barzani's relations with the USSR deteriorated when Moscow attempted to redirect the nationalist movement towards Iran and Turkey, two countries which Moscow wanted to destabilise on a priority basis. General Barzani, aware that a generalisation of the conflict would lead him into a strategic dead end, and taking into account the fact that the USSR was Iraq's main arms supplier, turned down every settlement.

1962 was a year of important advances for the Kurds, who held the whole of the north of Kurdistan from Zakho to the Iranian frontier. Apart from the fighting efficiency of the *peshmergas*, these advances could be explained by the ineffectual presence of Iraqi troops stuck in the south by the Kuwait crisis. The Kurdish militias, the *jash* (literally: 'the little donkeys'), recruited from the ranks of tribes hostile to Barzani, only had a limited effectiveness outside their home grounds. At the end of 1962, the Iraqi army was operating only in the plains, relying mainly upon the air force to defend the profitable parts of Kurdistan, such as the oil fields of Kirkuk.

This setback was to prove fatal to Qasim, who had brought about deep resentments in the army and amongst Arab nationalists. The opponents of the regime contacted the KDPI in April 1962 and promised, verbally, autonomy for Kurdistan. For Qasim, the end was near: on 9th February, at the end of a *coup d'état*, he was executed in front of television cameras after a summary 'trial'.

1963 to 1968: the first Ba'athist war and Marshal Aref's Arab nationalism

The coming to power of the Ba'ath party, the principal architect of the *coup d'état*, was marked by a particularly bloody communist witch-hunt. The new government quickly entered into negotiations with the KDPI through the intermediary of Jalal Talabani who was sent on a mission to Baghdad for the occasion. Contrary to the hopes of the Ba'ath party, Nasser gave his support to the Kurdish movement. This forced Baghdad, on 9th March 1963, and after some beating about the bush, to recognise the national rights of the Kurdish people on the basis of 'decentralisation'. In fact, this agreement was nothing more than the prelude to the rupture which occurred a month later, in April 1963, starting off the chain of events leading up to the war of June to November 1963.

The resumption of operations against General Barzani was announced officially on 10th June 1963 along with a plan for administrative reforms dividing Kurdistan into two provinces: Sulaymaniya and Kirkuk. The war started with the pillage of Kurdish towns by the Iraqi army. Hundreds of people were massacred in Sulaymaniya; their bodies were later discovered buried in a communal grave.

The assumption of power by the Ba'ath party led to two innovations: a massive strike in order to defeat the rebels by military means and a policy for the arabisation of the Kurdish regions. 40,000 people were expelled from the Kirkuk area (strategic because of its oil). The Kurds, up against the weight of a modern army, took refuge in the mountains to limit their losses.

On an international level, the intervention of a Syrian brigade against the Kurds strengthened Baghdad's position and further isolated the Kurds. The countries of the West, relieved by the fall of Qasim whom they considered pro-communist, had a *laissez-faire* attitude towards Baghdad and offered no protest. The USSR, concerned by the communist witch-hunt and its own loss of influence, started giving diplomatic support to the Kurds. But, confronted by violent Arab reactions, the USSR dropped its plan to place the Kurdish question on the agenda of the United Nations Security Council.

The Iraqi army's objective of destroying the Kurdish movement by military means proved to be an impossibility and this brought the war to a deadlock. It was only the fall of the Ba'ath party in November 1963, following internal divisions, which allowed the deadlock to be broken. The new strong man, General Aref, negotiated a cease-fire with Barzani in exchange for a vague promise of autonomy for Kurdistan. Barzani was fiercely criticised for this agreement by the leaders of the KDPI who had been kept away from the negotiations. The tensions between Jalal Talabani and Ibrahim Ahmed on one side, and Barzani on the other, soon became an open crisis. After having some of its delegates arrested, Barzani convened a congress of the KDPI in July 1964. Ibrahim Ahmed and Jalal Talabani, lacking the troops to oppose Barzani's 15,000 *peshmergas*, went into exile. They remained in Iran until 1965. General Barzani's take-over of the KDPI succeeded in marginalising the party's intellectuals, strengthening the personal aspect of the leadership and suppressing any reference to Marxism.

The cease-fire agreement, which was the immediate cause of KDPI's internal crisis, in fact only brought about an interlude of a few months, which allowed the two camps to rebuild their forces. The war started up again in April 1965 but, in the interval, General Barzani had managed to organise a Kurdish stronghold which remained inviolate until 1975.

Essentially rural and mountainous, the area within General Barzani's jurisdiction was contiguous with the Iraqi-Turkish frontier, and in part, with the Iranian frontier. In this area, despite an attempt at a parliament called the Revolutionary Council, Barzani had absolute power. From the beginning of the 1970s, his two sons, Idris and Masoud, became part of the limited circle of the leaders of the movement.

At the end of 1964, a number of limited engagements occurred between the *peshmergas* and the regular army, which was attempting to re-establish itself in Kurdistan. Winter delayed the outbreak of full-scale hostilities. These began in April when Aref launched an offensive at the head of what was virtually the whole Iraqi army (some 50,000 men). It was only Iranian aid which permitted the *peshmergas*, at last supplied with some heavy weaponry, to engage in position warfare, which continued through the winter of 1965-66. The Iranian aid, at the beginning, came from Iranian Kurdish sympathisers. However, it took on another dimension with the involvement of the government of Tehran during the summer of 1965, when the Shah decided to support Barzani despite the protests of the Arab states and of Baghdad.

At the beginning of 1966, Jalal Talabani, accompanied by other ex-leaders of the KDPI, joined the government in Baghdad. The government used these defectors to establish militias, some 20,000 strong, alongside the tribal *jash*. Under the leadership of Jalal Talabani, Ibrahim Ahmed, Ali Askari, Hilmi Charif and Omar Dababa, these militias confronted Barzani's men. This treachery, which was to cause deep hatreds, was justified by Talabani in terms of the 'tribal' nature of Barzani's movement. Behind these arguments lay a fierce power struggle in which personal rivalries played a more important role than ideology.

On the battle field, the violent confrontations of May-June 1966 allowed the Kurds to retain Mount Hendrin. The control of this area allowed access to the Hamilton road, linking Kurdistan with Iran, which was a vital means of communication for the Kurds. The fierce determination of the Kurds to stand their ground and their ability even to launch occasional counter attacks, forced the regular army to retreat.

This defeat, and the death of Marshal Aref a few days before the offensive, favoured the opening of negotiations which concluded, on 29th June 1966, with a cease-fire agreement and a recognition of the 'national rights of the Kurds'. In addition, an amnesty was decreed and Kurdish recognised as an official language. The final point marking Barzani's victory was the acceptance of the continuing existence of the *peshmergas*, albeit on a temporary basis. These agreements were more like an armed peace than a fundamental settlement of the Kurdish question. Nevertheless, from 1966 to 1969, the autonomy of Kurdistan did enable Barzani to conduct a policy, and even a broadly independent diplomacy. For instance, during the Arab-Israeli war (the Six-Day War), Barzani refused to send even a symbolic number of *peshmergas* to fight alongside the Iraqi army. Contacts were established between Barzani and the Israeli secret services, which probably supplied him with arms. Barzani also strengthened his relations with the Shah of Iran, who, in exchange, demanded and obtained from Barzani that he should cut off all aid to the Iranian Kurdish movements. In April to May 1968, Barzani even arranged the murder of two members of the Revolutionary Council, S. Moini and K. Chowbach, who wanted to organise a guerilla front in Iran from bases in Iraq.

The return to power of the Ba'ath party in 1968 was the starting point for a new war.

The second Ba'athist war and the agreements of 11th March 1970

At the outset, the Ba'ath party, which had left some very bad memories after its first period in power, seemed to prefer to make overtures rather than confrontations. Two Kurds loyal to Barzani were appointed as government ministers; but, at the same time, the KDPI dissidents Jalal Talabani and Ibrahim Ahmed attacked Barzani in their newspaper, *Al Nur* (The Light), and continued to receive government aid. Baghdad, in the hope of weakening its adversary, even pressured this group into attacks against Barzani's positions in Kurdistan.

Barzani's *peshmergas* struck the initial blow that unleashed the war. In March 1969 they struck at Kirkuk's oil installations. This intimidatory operation did not get the response they hoped for, since Baghdad sent four divisions to attack Kurdistan.

Despite its scale, the summer 1969 offensive did not achieve any decisive results. The government in Baghdad, faced with the danger of becoming bogged down, chose to negotiate. Despite some opposition from within the army, Saddam Hussein pushed through an agreement with Barzani which was finally signed on 11th March 1970.

During those few months of war, the Iraqi army conducted a number of operations against civilians. For instance, on 19th August 1969, the inhabitants of the village of Dokan in the Shaykhan district were asphyxiated when Iraqi soldiers lit fires at the entrance to the grotto in which they were hiding. Sixty-seven women, children and old people were killed. In September 1969, the village of Serija in the Zakho district was surrounded and then destroyed by a column of tanks. Amongst the Chaldaean population not a single person survived.

According to a report of the Economic and Social Council of the United Nations, which held an inquiry in Kurdistan in October 1970, 300 villages were affected by the war, 40,000 houses were destroyed and 300,000 people were left homeless.

In the short term, the agreement of 11th March 1970 led to the legalisation of the KDPI, the dismantling of Ibrahim Ahmed's militias, and a general amnesty. The agreement even provided for a census, which was to have served as the basis for setting the territorial limits of Kurdistan, but which was never organised. The region of Kirkuk, which Baghdad refused to include in Kurdistan, was already a principal bone of contention between the Ba'ath party and the Kurds. In 1972, the war was ready to start up again and an assassination attempt on General Barzani finally succeeded in breaking off relations between the two parties.

The conclusion of an Iraqi-Soviet friendship treaty, in April 1972, no longer left Barzani any choice in so far as any alliances were concerned. He renewed his lapsed contacts with the Shah of Iran. On the other hand, the American government, concerned by the pro-Soviet policy of Saddam Hussein, sent 16 million dollars to Barzani through the CIA between August 1972 and March 1975. As far as General Barzani was concerned, this relatively modest sum was, above all, a 'moral guarantee' of American support. What was to follow proved that General Barzani, by playing the

Americans as he had the British in earlier days, without understanding the cyclical aspect of external aid, was becoming extremely dependent on his allies. It was this that, following Iran's *volte-face*, brought about the collapse of 1975.

Following another assassination attempt on General Barzani in July 1972, the five remaining Kurdish ministers in the Baghdad government left for Kurdistan. From then on there was no free communication between Kurdistan and the rest of Iraq: the road from Baghdad to Kirkuk was staked out with security posts. In June 1973, General Barzani launched a public appeal to the United States (through the Washington Post) for aid for the Kurdish resistance. The only effect of this was to put a stop to the tentative beginnings of negotiations with Baghdad, without breaking the isolation of the Kurds, which was increasingly reinforced by the growing alliance between the Ba'ath party and the Iraqi CP. The attitude of the CP was such that it led to clashes with the KDPI in Kurdistan. Just as the war appeared to be on the point of breaking out again, the Israeli-Arab war of 1973 provided the Kurds with a few months respite. Although General Barzani did send a message of solidarity to Baghdad, he was envisaging a general war against the Iraqi army. This idea was finally abandoned on the advice of Kissinger, who feared that a *peshmerga* victory would, in time, result in problems for his Iranian ally.

Before committing himself to a trial of strength, Saddam Hussein attempted a manoeuvre to impose a status of autonomy, with or without the KDPI, and to rally prominent Kurds to the regime. The negotiations between the KDPI and Baghdad during the whole of the autumn of 1973 and up until the spring of 1974 resulted in deadlock, despite all the visits made to Baghdad by Barzani's son Idris. This setback was undoubtedly what Saddam Hussein wanted. It ended on 11th March with Baghdad's unilateral proclamation of a statute of autonomy for Kurdistan. The manoeuvre did succeed in rallying some prominent figures to the Ba'ath party. These included General Barzani's eldest son Ubeydullah, Aziz Aqraoui an ex-member of the politburo of the KDPI and, Hachem Aqraoui an ex-member of the central committee of the KDPI. Aziz Aqraoui then became the leader of a governmental KDPI, and remained so until 1980 when he went over to the opposition. The pro-governmental KDPI presented itself as a Ba'ath party for the Kurds and intended to act according to the same principles.

The 1974-75 war

The war began in February 1974 with artillery fire at the Iran-Iraq border, but the Iraqi army launched its real offensive in April 1974. The objective was to relieve the garrison at Zakho and this was achieved after fierce fighting. The air force played a key role, particularly the Soviet piloted Tupolev 22s which bombed Kurdish villages. The decisive attack against the Kurdish stronghold was launched during the summer of 1974: several hundred T62 tanks attacked Riwanduz and Qala Diza. Lacking anti-air-craft and anti-tank cover, the Kurdish forces were defeated at Qala Diza on 19th August and at Riwanduz on the 22nd.

The violence of the fighting had already driven tens of thousands of Kurds into exile. Iran agreed to shelter 110,000 of them at the border. Meanwhile, the last strategic obstacle in the form of Mount Hendrin and Mount Zozek, which dominate the Hamilton road, remained in the hands of the insurgents in September. 300 tanks and 30,000 infantrymen, the bulk of Iraq's fire power, was concentrated close to Mount Zozek for the final as-sault. After some extremely fierce fighting the Iraqi army was initially beaten back before taking control of Mount Zozek and the Chuman Valley on 3rd October 1974.

At the same time as pursuing its military offensives, the government in Baghdad was also setting up the institutions of the autonomous region, under the authority of Hachem Aqraoui. The situation in the north west was getting worse because of the Iraqi government's blockade of supplies, and, beyond the frontier, because of the Turkish army's clampdown on com-munications. Despite the opening up of a route to Badinan, the food and sanitary situations deteriorated during the autumn. At the time of the col-lapse of the Kurdish resistance, Doctor Alexander, a Dutch citizen who was working in the region, was caught and then hanged by the Iraqi army be-cause of his Jewish origins.

The spectacular reversal of alliances which was to bring about the defeat of the Kurdish resistance had already been brewing for several months. By aiding General Barzani, the Iranian government hoped to pressure the Iraqi government for a revision of the 1937 treaty concerning the Shatt al-Arab, and, more generally, for a diminution of Iraq's strength since it was the only Arab state able to compete with Iran as a regional power. At the beginning of 1975, the Shah of Iran felt that the time had come to reap the diplomatic advantage of his support for the Kurds. The Iraqi regime was also ready to come to an arrangement to end an interminable and costly war. In fact the initial contacts took place as early as the autumn of 1974 under the aegis of president Boumedienne and with the support of Anwar al-Sadat and King Hussein of Jordan. These dealings began to take a more concrete form at the 1975 OPEC summit in Algiers when Saddam Hussein and the Shah of Iran had a tête-à-tête which finally produced an agreement: strict and effective control of the border between the two countries, in exchange for which the terrestrial and fluvial border between Iran and Iraq was redefined to the benefit of Iran.

On the very day of the agreement, Iran pulled its artillery and anti-aircraft weapons out of Kurdistan. At that moment, the collapse of the Kurds seemed inevitable due to successive waves of intensive shelling and the general offensive launched by the Iraqi army. But the *peshmergas* put up a fierce fight and even managed to push back the government forces in the region of Riwanduz. At the Shah's request, Baghdad declared a unilateral cease-fire to give the fighters the chance to lay down their arms and seek refuge in Iran.

The evolution of the Kurdish parties in the 1980s

Up until 1975, the Kurdish political scene had been dominated totally by the KDPI and the personality of Barzani. After 1975, it underwent a complete break-up. There were conflicts between the numerous parties, which were often completely at odds with one another, and which lacked, at least until the Iran-Iraq war, any firm base within Kurdistan itself.

The Patriotic Union of Kurdistan (PUK), which emerged as an organisation in the summer of 1977, and became one of the principal rivals of the KDPI, had been created out of the fusion of a number of movements. The founding leaders of the PUK had one thing in common: their opposition to the personality of General Barzani. It was thus that Jalal Talabani, having been one of the protagonists in the 1964 crisis, before going over to Baghdad from 1966 to 1970, and then rejoining the KDPI as its representative in Syria, became the principal leader of the PUK. From Damascus, he organised a preparatory Committee for the Patriotic Union of Kurdistan which was also to include two other groups.

Komala was a Marxist-Leninist party formed in June 1970 outside of the Iraqi CP. Fearing reprisals from the KDPI, it remained underground until 1975. From June 1976, Komala started to organise small resistance groups.

The third party was the Socialist Party of Kurdistan whose leader Ali Askari had been a part of the Ibrahim Ahmed-Jalal Talabani group, and who retained excellent relations with the latter.

In August 1977, Jalal Talabani went to Kurdistan and, with Komala and the KSP, organised a new party: the PUK. The Socialist Party of Kurdistan joined and became the Revolutionary Union of Kurdistan. The Komala supplied the PUK with many of its troops, but Jalal Talabani dominated its political direction.

From the very first, the PUK was suspected of having a policy directed against the KDPI, and of negotiating with Baghdad to get an advantage over its principal rival. In 1978 there were violent clashes in the Badinan region between the *peshmergas* of the PUK and those of the KDPI. A number of activists, including Ali Askari, were killed and the KDPI accused the PUK of wanting to dislodge it from its positions.

A cease-fire agreement between Baghdad and the PUK, with Ghassemlou's Iranian PDK acting as intermediary, was concluded in October 1983.

From December 1983 to October 1984, the PUK negotiated its membership of the National Progressive Front (Ba'ath party) and collaborated with the government to resist Iranian attacks. At that time, the government only controlled the towns and the main roads of Kurdistan, the rest was in the hands of the *peshmergas*. In the end, the PUK was unable to conclude an agreement with Baghdad.

The KDPI was reborn in 1976 under the leadership of Idris and Masud Barzani. The party had a new Marxist-Leninist line, and supported Khomeini because of his anti-imperialist policy. In fact, a fresh alliance with the new government in Tehran was being re-created, at the same time as the Iranian KDP was working alongside the PUK, which was very opposed to the Barzani-led KDPIraq. An Iraqi National Democratic Front was formed on 28th November 1980 with the Iraqi CP, which was once more in opposition to the Ba'athist regime and had sought refuge in Kurdistan.

A number of small Islamic parties also began to appear during the 1980s. These movements arose out of the Iranian Revolution and were formed by *Sunnis* (who are largely in the majority amongst the Kurds of Iraq). The leader of the Kurdish Hizbullah was a brother of General Barzani, Shaikh Khalid Barzani. The most important movement was the Islamic Army of Kurdistan. The third party called itself the Islamic Movement of Iraqi Kurdistan.

In November 1986, the PUK and the KDPI jointly signed an agreement in Tehran with the Iranian regime. The rapprochement between the two groups accelerated after the tragedy at Halabja (Iraq) in March 1988, where 5,000 civilians were killed in a gas attack. An Iraqi Kurdistan Front was formed on 2nd May 1988. Apart from the PUK and the KDPI, the Front included the Socialist Party of Kurdistan, the Kurdish branch of the Iraqi Communist Party and the Popular Democratic Party of Kurdistan.

The settlement of a cease-fire agreement between Iran and Iraq in August 1988 had two consequences for the Kurds; the end of the Iranian alliance and the complete availability of the Iraqi army. The Iraqi army launched an extremely violent offensive against the Kurdish provinces on the border with Turkey from 25th August until 15th September. This huge operation mobilised 60,000 Iraqi soldiers and a large number of aircraft. 478 villages were destroyed and 77 villages gassed in the attack which caused the flight of around 100,000 of the region's 150,000 inhabitants. A reign of terror was established.

Social conditions in Kurdistan

Iraqi Kurdistan is a rich land which, despite deforestation, is still well timbered in parts. The climate is rainy and several rivers, including the Diyala and the Greater Zab, irrigate the country. With an area of only 17 per cent of the territory of Iraq (74,000 square kilometres), Kurdistan's population density is higher than that of the rest of the country. Despite imprecise figures, it is estimated that 25 per cent of the population of Iraq is Kurdish. An evaluation in 1975 gave a figure of around 3 million Kurds out of a total population of 11 million. Despite Baghdad's official recognition of a Kurdish minority, there has never been a census (although one was provided for in the 1970 agreements). Furthermore, the 'autonomous region of Kurdistan' recognised by Baghdad only corresponds to half of the lands that the nationalists claim have a majority Kurdish population.

Moreover, a large number of Kurds live outside Kurdistan: 300,000 in Baghdad; 100,000 in the south of Iraq, most of whom were forcibly transferred in the mid 1970s. On the other hand, there are more than 250,000 Arabs living in Kurdistan, most of them in the towns.

The population is still 50 per cent rural, but the nomads have almost totally disappeared because of the economic changes and, above all, war. The towns are traditionally areas of mixed population: Turkmens, Arabs and Kurds often live together without any problem. The most important urban agglomeration is Kirkuk with 580,000 inhabitants. Sulaymaniya has a population of 800,000. It is more typically Kurdish and is the real urban centre of Iraqi Kurdistan. This commercial town, once very prosperous, is situated in the middle of an area of intensive agriculture. Finally, Arbil, the capital of the autonomous region, has less of an urban tradition.

Baghdad's economic policy towards Kurdistan has been to marginalise the region. From 1970 to 1974 it received only 7 to 12 per cent, depending on the year, of developmental aid. Out of 150 government projects during this period, only four were in Kurdistan. Iron ore is extracted in Kurdistan, but the iron and steel works which facilitate economic take off were constructed in Arabic Iraq. In the same way, the oil from Kirkuk is refined outside Kurdistan in Hamman al-Alil, despite the 20 per cent extra cost.

In the agricultural domain, tobacco production, although a cultivation specific to Kurdistan, is subject to a national state monopoly, which imposes tight restrictions on production and prices.

However, Kurdistan's essential resource is oil. In the 1960s the oil from Kirkuk, Khanaqin and Aïn Zalek made up 80 per cent of Iraq's total production. That figure then fell to 70 per cent, but it still amounted to half the Iraqi state's revenue for that period. From 1964, the Iraqi government started a process of nationalisation which, to begin with, only targeted those oil-rich areas that had not already been exploited. The nationalisation of foreign companies began in the first years after the Ba'ath regime came to power (1st June 1972). By 1973, the Iraqi government had effective control of 85 per cent of the production. The increase of the price of oil in 1973 led to the doubling of Iraq's national income. It was this abundance of resources that permitted the struggle against the KDPI to be renewed in 1974.

In the cultural field Baghdad has often sought to revive the freedom enjoyed by the Kurdish minority. For instance in 1979, a university was created in Sulaymaniya and a Kurdish academy founded in Baghdad, although it was subsequently closed down in 1979. As for the university, it was later moved to Arbil and renamed the Salahadin University. From 1970 to 1983, 28 Kurdish periodicals were published: two in Kirkuk, six in Arbil, four in Sulaymaniya and sixteen in Baghdad. Iraqi radio also began broadcasting in Kurdish (as well as in Syriac and Turkoman).

On the other hand, from 1981 onwards, the Kurdish schools of Kirkuk, Khanaqin, Mosul and Dohuk only taught in Arabic.

In 1983, at the height of the war against Iran, the government made some overtures to the Kurds. For instance the autonomous region became the 'autonomous region of Kurdistan' again. In March 1983, the Kurdish publishing and cultural centre was revived and, a month later, a decree postponed the compulsory tuition of Arabic to the upper forms. In July 1983, just as the Barzani *peshmergas* were conducting joint attacks with the Pasdaran, Kurdish cultural festivals were being held in the principal towns of Kurdistan.

These occasional short-term shows of openness must not overshadow the real cultural discrimination. The number of students is distinctly less than the national average. In 1971-72, Kurdish students made up 6 per cent of the total attending Iraqi universities.

The Kurds are distinctly under-represented within the administration. In the military academy for the training of officers and in the police academy, Kurdish students make up less than 2 per cent of the total. Similarly, there are only ten diplomats of Kurdish extraction out the 500 who represent Iraq.

The adoption of Iraqi nationality is refused to Kurds whose families have sometimes lived in Iraq for several generations, whereas, in the context of the pan-Arabic ideology of the Ba'ath party, naturalisation for Arabs is facilitated by domicile or marriage.

The policies of Baghdad towards Kurdistan

The status of the autonomous region

The autonomy law, which came out of the agreements of 11th March 1970, established a new status for Kurdistan within the framework of the constitution. It specified, in article 5, that Iraq is a part of the Arab Nation but that the people of Iraq consist of two communities: Arab and Kurdish. The rights of the Kurdish minority were recognised and protected within the limits of national unity.

Its general rules were defined by decision no 228 of the High Council of the Revolution which provided for: a Kurdish vice-president, Kurdish speaking Kurdish officials in districts with a Kurdish majority and the absence of discrimination in public office. According to law no 33 of 1974, which completed the statute of autonomy, Kurdistan includes the three provinces of Sulaymaniya, Arbil and Dohuk. The town of Arbil is the administrative centre of the autonomous region. In 1983, Saddam Hussein proclaimed it the summer capital following the population's contributions to the war against Iran (these included gold and jewellery). The law also stipulated that Kurdish would be an official language alongside Arabic in the region. For the Kurds, Arabic and Kurdish were to become languages used at every level of teaching.

Essentially there are two institutions which are peculiar to Kurdistan: a legislative council and an executive council. According to law no 33 of 1974, the Legislative Council of the autonomous region has the following jurisdictions:

1) the adoption of laws necessary for the progress of the region and for the development of local social, cultural and economic services within the context of the general policy of the state;

2) the adoption of laws connected with the promotion of the culture, the particularisms and the national traditions of the citizens of the region;

3) the adoption of laws connected with non-official organisations and local businesses;

4) the adoption of detailed plans, prepared by the Executive Council, for projects in the economic and social spheres, as well as for development projects in the realms of education, health and employment, in accordance with the imperatives of the central general plan of the state;

5) the approval of the ordinary budget of the region after its adoption by the Executive Council;

6) the introduction of amendments to the ordinary budget of the region after its adoption and within the limits of the allocated amounts and the stated objectives, on condition that this be in accordance with the prevailing laws;

7) discussions with and questioning of the Executive Council on issues relating to its jurisdictions;

8) the establishment of the rules of procedure of the Council.

The composition of the Legislative Council was set by law no 56 of 15th March 1980. Its members are elected by direct universal suffrage and by secret ballot, with one person elected for every 30,000 inhabitants (58 members in the 1983 elections). In practice, the Ba'ath party controls the majority of the seats and the pro-governmental KDP is represented. The Legislative Council holds two sessions a year, one of which can be prolonged by one month, by decree of the president of the republic or by a majority decision of the members of the Council. The Legislative Council proposes and votes on laws applicable to the autonomous region and can censure the Executive Council. The Executive Council is the executive organ of the Legislative Council. It consists of a president, a vice-president and nine general secretaries. It should be noted that irrigation remains a matter for the central government in Baghdad. The Executive Council handles the everyday administration of the autonomous region and prepares an annual report for the president of the republic.

Powers are distributed between region and state according to the principle of the Central state's overall jurisdiction, with the exception of particular provisions of the law which give jurisdiction to the region. The president of the Executive Council takes part in the Council of Ministers. In August 1986, Saddam Hussein attended the first session of the Legislative Council for the first time and gave a speech which was favourable towards autonomy.

Nevertheless, in practice, the Executive Council is always nominated by Saddam Hussein. Although the Legislative Council has been elected since 1980, it has little influence. Baghdad decides on its overall budget and the central government can overturn its decisions. In addition, in 1986, the government in Baghdad had a law voted in requiring election candidates to be sponsored by the Ba'ath party. In another connection, there was no decrease in the number of arbitrary arrests and tortures during this period. The restoration of Iraq's military position in 1988 allowed Saddam Hussein to abandon his policy of openness.

The deportation of populations

From 1963, following the overthrow of the first Ba'ath regime, Aref's regime attempted to institute a policy of arabisation of Kurdistan. Incentives were offered to the Arab people in order to encourage them to settle in the borderlands of Kurdistan. Afterwards, this policy intensified with a clear determination to arabise the Kurdish territories.

After the 1974-75 war, the Iraqi government deported the Kurdish and Assyrian populations to the deserts in the south of Iraq. Arabisation was introduced in three regions: Sinjar, Kirkuk and Khanaqin. Kurdish villages were destroyed and the Agricultural Reform Commission only gave title-deeds of properties to Arab peasants. After a few years, some Kurds did return to Kurdistan but, lacking the authorisation to stay in their villages, they settled in the towns of Sulaymaniya, Arbil and Dohuk. New towns, purpose built for the occasion and adjoining military bases, received the refugees. The difficult living conditions led to demonstrations in 1978 and 1979.

Meanwhile, the Iraqi government had begun to empty the frontier areas of their Kurdish population. Between June 1978 and April 1979, 250,000 villagers were relocated to the new towns. On 26th June 1989, an official declaration by the Iraqi government recognised that the purpose of these population movements was to create a 30 kilometre wide band of depopulated territory along the 120 kilometre frontier with Turkey and Iran.

The war against Iran put a brake on these territorial operations. Then, in 1985, after the failure of the negotiations with Talabani, the Iraqi government announced a plan for population resettlements affecting 500,000 people. Traditional villages were destroyed and populations installed close to roads and military bases in order to give the government greater control over them.

In June 1989, Qala Diza, to the north of Sulaymaniya and 10 kilometres from the Iranian border, was evacuated by force. In fact, the 50,000 inhabitants had received the order to leave, with only those belongings that they could carry, on 29th March. The population refused to comply and sent a delegation to Saddam Hussein. Mullah Muhammad Delgai, who led the delegation, was imprisoned. Qala Diza was evacuated finally in June after the army had surrounded it. The town was razed to the ground and its population rehoused in camps at Arbil and Sulaymaniya.

The number of villages that have been wiped off the map varies considerably according to the different estimates (there are no official figures). Kurdish sources give 3,500 villages destroyed out of a total of 5,000, or approximately 70 per cent. The American State Department quoted a lower figure of approximately 1,200, but recognised that the estimates were arbitrary. The Kurdish mountains are now practically empty, and this presents the *peshmergas* with logistical problems. For example, the survivors of Halabja have been relocated to a new town, some 20 kilometres from the old one, which is called Saddamite Halabja in honour of Saddam Hussein.

The inhabitants of the new towns are often unemployed and in a difficult situation, both materially and psychologically. The state of dependence thus created allows the government to recruit militiamen or informers for the secret police. Of the 500,000 displaced people, those that remained went to live in Sulaymaniya, Arbil or Dohuk. Others were transferred to camps in the south of Iraq. Four camps have been cited: Ar, Nughrat, Salman, and Mutba. Finally, in the spring of 1989, the Iraqi regime also took measures against the city dwelling Kurds. They were prevented from buying or building houses, and those inhabitants who had taken up residence after 1975 had to be registered by the police.

The use of chemical weapons

The chemical attack on the Kurds in August 1988 was not the first time that Saddam Hussein's government had used gas. There were similar bombardments in 1983, in the war against Iran. Despite protests by the United Nations in March 1984, Iraq continued to use this weapon on a regular basis, to the point when Iran estimated that 50,000 people had been killed or injured by gas between 1983 and 1988. In January 1988, the Iraqi government again categorically denied that the Iraqi army had used chemical weapons.

In fact, Iraq began its massive toxic gas production programme in 1974 (this does not contravene the 1925 Geneva Protocol, which only condemns its use). Since 1985, Iraq has produced large quantities of mustard gas and two different types of nerve gas. This puts Iraq at the head of the countries of the third world in so far as its chemical arsenal is concerned.

On 15th and 16th April 1987, Iraq launched gas attacks against Kurdish villages in the region of Sulaymaniya and Arbil. There were 300 people killed and injured. According to certain sources, the 380 survivors who went for treatment in government hospitals were executed in military camps at Arbil.

There were other attacks in May, June and September 1987. It was the bombing of the town of Halabja, close to the Iranian border, on 16th and 17th March which finally drew international attention. The presence of television crews showing the corpses of the victims ensured that this tragedy would have international repercussions. It was the capture of the town by the Iranians, with the help of the *peshmergas*, that led to the gas attack by Iraqi aeroplanes. The Iranian government considered this to be a good opportunity to discredit its adversary and was the first to protest to the UN. The specialist sent by this international body concluded his report by attesting that the injured had been affected by chemical weapons and that most of them were civilians. When it was attacked, the town had a population of over 70,000 people because of the refugees from nearby Kurdish villages. It was difficult to calculate the number of victims, although it has been estimated that 5,000 were killed.

Despite the protests of the UN (the Security Council condemned the use of gas on 9th May and 26th August 1988), the Iraqi government continued to gas Kurdish villages, particularly during the month of September, causing several thousand deaths.

Turkey, which was taking in numerous refugees, was to adopt a position very close to that of Iraq by refusing to acknowledge that gas had been used against the Kurds. Kurdish doctors who examined refugees concluded that they were suffering from recognised illnesses and not from exposure to gases. In 1982, the two states signed an agreement authorising Turkey to pursue the *peshmergas* onto Iraqi territory. Moreover, Turkey's main oil supplier was Iraq; and for Iraq, Turkey remains an important creditor. In September 1988, the Iraqi and Turkish governments simultaneously rejected a proposal made by Pérez de Cuéllar, the Secretary General of the UN, to send a team of experts to the two countries.

The Ambassador of the Arab League to the United Nations, reacting to the condemnation that Iraq had been subjected to at the UN in August and September 1988, argued that the 1925 Geneva Protocol was not applicable to the case in point. In fact, he pointed out that the accord was concerned with wars between states and not the internal activities of a sovereign state.

There is no military justification for the use of gas by the Iraqi army. As the Iraqi Defence Minister observed, quite correctly, during a press conference on 15th September 1988: in a mountainous terrain, gases are not a 'logical' weapon. In fact, gases have mainly been used to create panic and to throw hundreds of thousands of Kurds onto the roads. According to Saddam Hussein's way of thinking, this would greatly facilitate the arabisation programme, which remains the objective of his policy in Kurdistan.

The refugees

The war in Iraqi Kurdistan brought about the departure into exile of numerous Iraqi Kurds. Their total number has been estimated at 400,000, or 10 per cent of the Kurdish population in Iraq. Approximately 370,000 of these refugees live in Iran, 28,000 in Turkey, 3,000 in Pakistan and 2,500 in Western Europe (1990 estimates).

There have been Kurdish refugees in Iran since 1971. There was a substantial increase in the number of refugees following the gas attacks of 1988-89. The present population of 370,000 is distributed among 23 refugee camps situated in Iranian Kurdistan. The Iraqi Kurds do not enjoy refugee status and do not have the benefit of the protection of the international organisations. Health conditions are bad and aggravated by the harsh climate.

In August and September 1988, more than 55,000 Iraqi Kurds fled Kurdistan for Turkey. The Turkish authorities refused to grant them refugee status. Turkey had ratified the United Nations Convention on the status of refugees in 1951, following events intervening in Europe. Turkey, at least in theory, was nothing but a region of transit for the refugees while they waited to be granted asylum in a third country.

Since September 1988, the Iraqi government has decreed five amnesties for political opponents, two of which were specially for the Kurds. Nonetheless, at the end of 1988, Iraq refused to allow the International Committee of the Red Cross to help in the repatriation of the Kurdish refugees in Turkey. According to the Iraqi government's figures, 7,644 people benefited from the amnesty of the 6th September 1988, a total of 8,129 people for all of the amnesties. In fact, the number of people who went back to Iraq was greater, in the region of 10,000.

Since September 1988, repatriations of Kurds have been undertaken on a bilateral basis, without any intervention by the specialised international organisations, and Amnesty International drew attention to forced repatriations in a report published in June 1990. Furthermore, the government in Baghdad did not carry out the amnesties and, there were numerous cases of 'disappearance', torture or execution among those 'amnestied'.

4. The Kurds of Iran

Simko's revolt

The dismemberment of the Ottoman Empire combined with the weakness of the Iranian state during the 1920s opened the way for the rise in nationalist feelings in Iranian Kurdistan.

The first movement's prime mover was Simko, the son of Mohammad Agha, the chief of the Shikak tribe.

After his elder brother was assassinated in 1907 by the Governor of Tabriz, Simko, who avowed a fierce hatred of the Persians from then on, sought alliances with the Turks and the British. In 1918, Simko refused to join the Armenians in resisting the Turks and assassinated the Assyrian patriarch Mar Shimoun. In the same year he conquered the area between Lake Urmiya and the Turkish border. The acts of violence committed against the Assyrian community earned Simko his solid reputation as a brigand, as far as the Western powers were concerned. This aggravated his isolation. First of all, the Tehran government attempted to get rid of this annoying leader by sending him a booby-trapped parcel which killed one of his brothers. In the summer of 1919, Simko took the town of Rezaieh which was immediately ransacked. Then, the Brigade of Persian Cossacks, led by a Russian officer Colonel Filipov, attacked Simko's forces which were defeated but not destroyed. Negotiations followed.

The situation was stable until October 1921, when, threatened by the arrival of new troops from Tehran, Simko preferred to take the initiative and seized the small town of Mahabad. The 400 gendarmes in residence were massacred and, in the ensuing pillage, several Kurdish notables were killed. Simko's behaviour alienated him from the whole of the local population. Nevertheless, Simko was at the height of his power and, on several occasions, managed to defeat the troops that were sent against him.

Although no ordinary tribal leader, Simko lacked any clearly defined policies. There was no doubt about his nationalist sentiments but, in all the territories that he controlled, he never sought to establish an administration which could have underpinned his ambitions to create an independent state.

After Reza Khan came to power, Simko sought support from Great Britain in order to avoid a brutal confrontation with the new Iranian regime. Following some preliminary discussions, the British government finally refused to negotiate with Simko. From then on, the Kurdish movement was marginalised and under sentence of death. The Turkish-Persian accord of 25th October 1922 completed Simko's isolation by bringing an end to Turkish aid. The decisive battle took place on 25th July 1922 at Shakar

Yazi. Faced with a more organised and better armed adversary, Simko's troops were crushed. Out of the 10,000 men he started off with, Simko was left with only a thousand, all from his tribe, with which to continue an ever more unequal struggle.

Simko left for Iraq, then Turkey. His long odyssey finally came to an end in 1930, when Reza Shah made him governor of Uchnovieh — and then had him assassinated a few days later.

The Mahabad republic

The Mahabad republic remains the only example of a fragile Kurdish independence. It lasted from 22nd January 1946 until December of the same year. One can only understand how an area of total autonomy could have been created in part of Kurdistan during the post Second World War period in its historical context. The potentiality for this independence arose out of the joint Soviet-British occupation of Iran between August 1941 and 1945. The Mahabad region acted as a buffer zone between the territories occupied by the two allied powers. But, while the British objective was to keep Iran territorially intact in order to provide an obstacle to Soviet expansionism, Moscow wanted to gain new zones of influence through the dismemberment of Iran. The reunification of Azerbaijan was a priority for Moscow, but the Kurds could also be a factor in the break-up of Iran.

In November 1941, two Azeri Soviet officers invited some thirty Kurdish notables to Baku. Amongst them was the future leader of the Mahabad republic, Qazi Muhammad. The latter had previously attempted to make contact with the British, but it was the logic of geopolitics rather than a political sympathy that was to lead him into a close co-operation with the Soviets. In Baku, Bakirov, the president of the Praesidium of the republic of Azerbaijan, avoided making any concrete promise to the Kurds, remaining, on the contrary, very circumspect; whereas he pledged total support for the demand for the reunification of Azerbaijan under Soviet protection.

During the first years of the allied occupation, Qazi Muhammad quickly asserted himself as a respected leading citizen of Mahabad. Born in 1900, he came from one of the town's most important families, and was predominant, because of his education (he spoke English, French, Turkish and Arabic) amongst the local politicians.

The Komala, Komala Jiwanewey Kurd (The Kurdish Resurrection Movement) was created in September 1942, at a time when there was total anarchy in a Kurdistan which was not obviously subject to any of the occupying powers. The movement was founded by fifteen or so of Mahabad's leading figures and was soon able to extend its audience beyond the boundaries of the town by recruiting tribal chiefs. The exception was *Shi'ite* Kurdistan where it was unable to take root. In May 1943, the inhabitants stormed Mahabad's police station and, from that moment on, the town's total independence was established. Qazi Muhammad did not join the Komala until October 1944 but he very quickly became the dominant personality of the movement. Between August and October, the Komala transformed itself into the KDP-Iran (Kurdistan Democratic Party of Iran). The party's programme was still quite moderate: the autonomy of Kurdistan within the framework of Iran and the recognition of cultural rights. Nevertheless the situation evolved rapidly in the shift of perspective brought about by the end of the war.

In September 1945, a second trip to Baku enabled the leaders of the KDP-Iran to reassure themselves of the USSR's support. The USSR, however, had scarcely any intention of respecting the agreements, which provided for the evacuation of Iran not more than six months after the end of hostilities. The autonomy of Azerbaijan was announced on 13th December 1945; two days later it was the Kurds' turn to proclaim the autonomy of Mahabad. In fact, Qazi Muhammad was maintaining relations with the Tehran government, and affirmed his desire for a statute of autonomy and not independence. Confident of Soviet support, Qazi Muhammad declared 'The Autonomy of the Republic of Kurdistan' on 22nd January 1946 in the presence of Mullah Mustafa Barzani. The latter, recently arrived from Iraqi Kurdistan, was soon to be at the head of the ephemeral republic's army, with the rank of general.

A government, consisting mainly of merchants and tribal chiefs, was formed immediately. Soviet aid was very parsimonious, and despite the presence of Soviet officers for the training of the traditional Kurdish army, there was still an absence of heavy weapons.

Furthermore the two republics, Kurdish and Azeri, were to clash over the delimitation of their respective territories. Certain towns, often populated with a minority of Kurds, were incorporated into Azerbaijan, to the detriment of the Mahabad republic. The Soviets became the arbiters of the conflict and concluded a treaty between the Azeri and Kurdish republics on 23rd April 1946. The negotiations between Tehran and Tabriz ended in June 1946 with an agreement in which the Azeris acknowledged themselves to be, at least nominally, an integral part of Iran, without making mention of the Kurdish republic.

The evacuation of Iran by the Soviet army in May 1946 was the signing of the death warrant for the Mahabad republic, despite a cease-fire agreement in May 1946. Tehran began its offensive in November 1946 with the recapture of Azerbaijan. This was facilitated by the population's hatred of Pishevari's Stalinist regime. Mahabad's Kurdish chiefs surrendered and Qazi Muhammad was arrested and hanged, along with a number of the other leaders, in March 1947. Mullah Mustafa Barzani and several hundred of his men managed to get to the USSR.

During the few months of its existence, the Mahabad republic established the foundations of a Kurdish administration. Thus, for the first time, education was officially in Kurdish, and a Kurdish press began to develop. In contrast to Azerbaijan, the economic infrastructure was untouched; there was no nationalisation and the government respected fundamental liberties.

As was so often the case during the course of the history of the Kurds in the 20th century, the fall of the Mahabad republic resulted from the cessation of aid from a regional power, in this case the USSR, which was finally satisfied by an oil concession in the north of Iran. In addition, certain tribal chiefs, who depended on tobacco for their livelihood, became concerned by the drop in their income due to the loss of the Iranian market, and turned against the Mahabad republic in 1946. Nevertheless, the Mahabad republic has remained an important moment in the political history of Kurdistan, in particular with the formation of the KDP-Iran, and via Barzani, the KDP-Iraq; the parties which have been at the heart of the nationalist struggle in their two countries up until the present day.

The evolution of the Kurdish movement from 1946 to 1980

With the disappearance of the Mahabad republic, the Kurdish nationalist movement had, in practice, been dismantled. The KDP-Iran was rebuilt during the early 1950s when Dr. Mossadeq was coming to power. At this time, the KDP-Iran assumed a very marked left wing stance with leaders such as Ghani Bulourian and Aziz Yussefi. At the 1952 elections, six years after the fall of the Mahabad republic, the KDP-Iran candidate got between 80 and 91 per cent of the votes in the town of Mahabad and its surrounding regions. These elections were annulled by the government and a religious leader was appointed as parliamentary deputy. In the same year, the KDP-Iran led the peasants of Bokan in an uprising against the gendarmes and the major land-owners. The movement quickly gained strength but was put down by the Shah's army with the support of certain tribal chiefs.

After Mossadeq's fall on 19th August 1953, following a *coup d'état* organised by the CIA, the repression of the Kurds increased. In 1955, Iran, Iraq, Turkey and Pakistan signed the Baghdad Pact. Although it was mainly directed against Soviet expansionism, it also concerned the Kurds.

In the first instance, the repression affected the Jwanro, a Kurdish tribe from the north of Kirmanshah who had managed to retain a form of local autonomy, favoured by their proximity to the Iraqi border. The signing of the Baghdad Pact encouraged the Shah to launch his troops against the Jwanro on 4th February 1956. They abandoned the fortress that had been a symbol of their independence and sought refuge in the mountains.

The KDP-Iran had supported Mossadeq, and they too were badly affected by the repression which followed his overthrow. With its central organisation destroyed, the party reorganised itself based on local committees. Between 1955 and 1958, Abdul Rahman Ghassemlou established himself as leader of the party and worked in close collaboration with the Iranian communist party (the Tudeh).

The KDP-Iran then experienced a decade of internal ravages. The party's second congress, which was held in Iraq in 1964, saw the return of General Barzani as the central figure of the Kurdish movement, and certain delegates, such as A. R. Ghassemlou, were excluded from the debates. In fact, the disagreements were mainly the result of the emerging co-operation between the Iraqi KDP, under General Barzani, and the Shah of Iran. A 'revolutionary committee' was set up separately from the KDP-Iran, with A. R. Ghassemlou as one of its leaders. Relations between the two movements deteriorated rapidly. In 1968, Barzani's *peshmergas* prevented a number of members of the committee from escaping to Iraq: as a result five of them were to die. Another, Sulaiman Muini, was arrested and executed by Barzani's men and his corpse handed over to the Iranian army.

After its first congress, the KDP-Iran's programme remained relatively constant: the autonomy of Kurdistan within a democratic Iran. Rejecting independence, the KDP-Iran wanted to create a socialist society, close to the Soviet model. Inspired by Marxism, the KDP-Iran remained resolutely secular. During the course of the years, whilst it retained its popular slant, the KDP-Iran all but ceased referring to Marxism.

Taking advantage of the weakness of the KDP-Iran at the end of the 1960s, a new party emerged. It was Maoist inspired and known as the Komala. Created in 1969 by extreme left wing students, it was opposed to the Tudeh and therefore to the USSR. From 1972, the party propagandised in student and working class circles, but its activities tailed off somewhat after 1975 following a wave of arrests. After a large number of activists were freed in 1975, the Komala, which was in the middle of a structural reorganisation, was able to hold its first congress in the same year. The party's programme had evolved from its Maoist beginnings. The autonomy of Kurdistan within a socialist Iran remained as the goal, however co-operation with the Tudeh had also become desirable.

The Kurdish movement after the Islamic revolution

The collapse of the Imperial government in 1978 allowed Kurdistan to acquire a *de facto* autonomy. After the Shah went into exile, the KDP-Iran sent representatives to Tehran to recognise the new regime and to negotiate the status of Kurdistan as an autonomous province. Ayatollah Khomeini refused to hear of an autonomy which, according to him, was contrary to Islamic principles. The failure of the talks was followed by the authorities retaking strict control of other minorities, notably the Turkmens in April 1979.

The *pasdaran* (Revolutionary Guards) were sent to Kurdistan following Ayatollah Khomeini's proclamation, in August 1979, of a *fatwa* declaring a holy war 'against the atheist people of Kurdistan'. The KDP-Iran, which had ceased being clandestine on 3rd March 1979, became illegal once more. In Kurdistan, there was a low turn-out (less than 50 per cent) for the constitutional referendum of 15th November; there were also bloody clashes with the police. Following the poll, Ayatollah Khomeini made overtures to the KDP-Iran within the context of preparations for a plan for the status of minorities. The negotiations stumbled over the question of the disarmament of the KDP-Iran, which was a prerequisite demanded by Tehran but rejected by the Kurdish movement. In March 1980, the KDP-Iran had the opportunity to assess its influence on the population during the parliamentary elections. It obtained 80 per cent of the votes in Kurdistan. This popular recognition did not stop the president of the republic, Bani Sadr, from sending his troops against the *peshmergas* just one month later. The *peshmergas* were forced to seek refuge in the mountains.

This military offensive allowed the government to install *Shi'ite* clergy in key administrative posts, despite the fact that 75 per cent of the population was *Sunni* (with the exception of the Kermanshah region). The dogmatism of the revolutionary clergy quickly led to disturbances among the population, particularly as the clergy had taken the side of the large landowners, who were often members of the revolutionary 'committees', against the peasants. In Kurdistan, the Shah's downfall had sparked off a wave of occupations of large farms with absentee landlords. The landlords, in alliance with the *pasdaran*, had their lands restored to them following a series of clashes with the peasants.

Following the 1980 legislative elections, the KDP-Iran experienced a schism which weakened it at a crucial moment. The divergence arose from an evaluation of Ayatollah Khomeini's regime. A group led by Ghani Bulurian (a Marxist intellectual who had survived the Shah's prisons) reproached Ghassemlou for his links with Baghdad, and recommended, on the contrary, the recognition of Ayatollah Khomeini's regime. This faction broke away from the movement. This strategic choice, patterned on that of the Tudeh party, presupposed that the Islamic regime was conducting an 'anti-imperialist' (read 'anti-American') struggle and had therefore to be treated with consideration: Kurdish autonomy, in particular, could only be obtained by peaceful means. When Ayatollah Khomeini's regime liquidated the Tudeh party in May 1983, the validity of Ghani Bulurian's strategy was brought sharply into question. Tudeh's members themselves sought refuge in the region held by the Kurds, where the party was able to reorganise itself. Before long expelled from the towns by the *pasdaran*, the KDP-Iran tried to establish an autonomous territory in the heart of the regions under its control. It set up an embryonic administration, with particular attention to education in Kurdish (text books were published at the end of 1981). To a certain extent, the aid provided by non-governmental French humanitarian organisations such as Médecins du Monde, Médecins sans Frontières, etc., which had set up small medical teams, replaced on a regular basis, from the end of 1981, made up for the absence of any medical infrastructure. The KDP-Iran also had a radio station which broadcast twice a day in Kurdish, Azeri and Persian. Relations with the Komala movement were extremely tense. There were military clashes between the two parties for the control of certain areas until 1982-83. From then on, faced with the threat of the Iranian army, confrontation between the two antagonists changed to co-operation.

The KDP-Iran's attempt to establish an autonomous Kurdistan, free from Tehran's jurisdiction, came to grief following a succession of Iranian army offensives beginning in 1983. With operation Dawn II, the Iranian army was able to seize the Hadj Omran area; a strategic height which dominates the oil fields of northern Iraq and which gave them the ability to stop communications between Piramshar and Riwanduz. The supply bases of the Kurds who had taken to the mountains were cut off, and the *peshmergas*, who had retreated there to escape the Turkish army's incursions onto Iraqi territory, were deprived of their sanctuary. In October 1983, during Dawn IV, the Iranian army made a breakthrough towards Panjwin and occupied the strategic heights of Iranian Kurdistan. From then on, the KDP-Iran no longer controlled any territory.

In January 1984, the party's fourth congress, in admitting its military setbacks, opted for a guerilla war avoiding any direct confrontations. The alliance with Baghdad was reaffirmed, since the KDP-I needed Iraq's help with logistics more than ever. The only party which still maintained good relations with the KDP-Iran was Talabani's PUK, which was then seeking a rapprochement with Baghdad. Finally, at the risk of becoming marginalised in Iran, the KDP-Iran joined the National Resistance Council on 27th October 1981. However, Masoud Rajavi, its president, had the founding of an Islamic republic written into his programme, which went against the KDP-Iran's secular principles. The Kurdish movement left the National Resistance Council in 1983 as a result of disagreements with Masoud Rajavi, the leader of the People's Mujahidin.

Thanks to its alliance with Baghdad, the KDP-Iran was able to set up its headquarters on Iraqi territory, not far from the Iranian frontier. After the cease-fire between Iraq and Iran in August 1988, A. R. Ghassemlou confirmed his readiness to negotiate with Tehran with regard to a statute of autonomy for Kurdistan. A first meeting, and a series of discussions took place in Vienna on 30th and 31st of December, followed by a second series

in the same town on 19th and 20th January 1989. This willingness to negotiate had created tensions at the heart of the KDP-Iran. Some factions had
even seceded in 1988. Jalal Talabani, the leader of the PUK, acted as intermediary between the two parties for the first series of discussions. The death
of Ayatollah Khomeini in June 1989 seemed to give a new impetus to the
negotiations, but on 13th July 1989, Abdul Rahman Ghassemlou and
Ghaderi Azar, his representative in Europe, were assassinated in Vienna.

A. R. Ghassemlou was born into an important family in 1930. The son
of the chief of a tribe from the north-east of Kurdistan, he sought refuge in
1949 first of all in France, then in Czechoslovakia where he studied economics. First as an activist, then as a member of the Tudeh party, he spent
fifteen years in Prague working as a lecturer in economics. He left the party
during the Prague Spring of 1968. When he returned to Iran in the autumn
of 1978, convinced of the impossibility of a military solution to the Kurdish
problem, Ghassemlou fell victim to the illusion that he could bring negotiations with the Iranian government to a satisfactory conclusion.

The inquiry clearly showed that the Iranian services were involved in the
assassination. Arrest warrants were issued for two Iranian diplomats who
had left Austrian territory. Nevertheless, the Austrian government was
above all anxious to remain uninvolved in the affair. The assassination left
the KDP-Iran rudderless.

The policy of the Iranian state in respect of the Kurds

Iran, in common with all states, distrusts nomads. The Iranian army was
used by Reza Shah, in the period between the wars, to settle those tribes
(most of them non-Kurdish) which had hitherto been itinerant, and to establish central government control of these populations. For certain Kurdish tribes, the consequences of this enforced settling were severe. The Jelali
tribe, with its territory split between the USSR, Iran and Turkey, was deported and massacred before the war. In 1941, only a few hundred members of the tribe, out of a total of some ten thousand, returned from the
centre of Iran where they had been deported. The Galbaghi tribe, deported
to Hamadan and the area around Isphahan, saw its lands occupied by
Turkish speakers and attempted, unsuccessfully, to rebel against the government. The end of nomadism and particularly of cross-border
nomadism, slowed down the traditional commercial channels, which
nonetheless continued with smuggling. Occasionally, a tribe found itself
divided between two countries, for example the Shikak (divided between
Turkey and Iran). In any case, the end of nomadism brought about a large
increase in the number of villages (approximately 7,500), and profound
modifications of the economic and social structures.

One of the major upheavals in the social situation of the region arose
from another government initiative of the 1960s. The agricultural reform

undertaken by the Shah led to the disappearance of the large landowners, who were, historically speaking, the heirs of the tribal chiefs. The policy of settling the nomads had brought about the confiscation of the lands of a tribe in favour of its leaders, the aghas, who then became large landowners (with more than 300 hectares per family), owning more than 60 per cent of the cultivated land. The medium size landowners (from 30 to 50 hectares), who were spared by the reform, managed to keep their lands, and from then on formed the majority.

Nevertheless, the tribal chiefs were not on a systematic collision course with the government. On the contrary, some of them allied themselves with Tehran in order to secure special privileges, such as grazing rights. In addition to this, mayors and parliamentary deputies were often either tribal chiefs or their heirs. Occasionally, the religious factor came into play. A number of tribes with *Shi'ite* chiefs (for instance at Qara Papag) were able to forge alliances with the state, on occasion against other tribes.

There has never been a programme of public investment in the Kurdish regions. The roads are in a deplorable state. The only one to be asphalted, and this only for strategic reasons, lies along the Iraqi border.

The social structures

The Kurds of Iran live in a mountainous region where the towns are often at an altitude of over 1,000 metres. The climate is continental with large variations in temperature, but often less arid than the other regions of Iran. The mountains cover 4 million hectares of the 125,000 square kilometres inhabited by the Kurds.

Because of the administrative divisions adopted by the Iranian government, the name Kurdistan only applies to the Sanandaj region, whereas a part of Azerbaijan and the south of Kermanshah province are also ethnically Kurdish.

Since the Iranian government does not publish any figures on Kurdish demography, only approximations are available. The Kurds make up an estimated 15 per cent of the population, or some 7 million people. The annual growth rate for the Kurdish population, which is more rural than the average, exceeds 2.8 per cent. Outside Kurdistan, there are important Kurdish populations in Goutchan and Dargaz in Khorasan province. They were transferred there by Shah Abbas at the beginning of the 17th century to defend the frontiers of the Persian Empire. There are approximately 600,000 of them. Furthermore, it should be noted that some 15 per cent of the inhabitants of Kurdistan are Persians or Azeris.

The population density of Kurdistan is twice that of the rest of the country. Kermanshah province is by far the most urbanised of the four provinces inhabited by the Kurds but, as in the rest of the country, the rate of urbanisation is accelerating. The birth rate tends to drop with urbanisation: in the countryside there is an average of six children per family, whereas in the towns this drops to five. The four principal Kurdish towns are Mahabad, Saqqez, Sanandaj and Kermanshah. Apart from its historic role in 1946, Mahabad is an important urban centre and road junction. Mahabad controls the Riwanduz-Tabriz road, which gives access to Iraqi Kurdistan. It is a town that has been inward looking for a long time, and which has few economic links apart from those with Azerbaijan and Mosul (in Iraq). Kermanshah is the capital of the province that bears its name. It experienced a period of spectacular development at the end of the 19th century, and remains today, with over a million inhabitants, the most important Kurdish urban centre. Its population is *Shi'ite*. Nomadism has now virtually disappeared, with the exception of a few small tribes.

Kurdistan's economy is still largely based on agriculture: more than half the population lives off the land, which provides most of the wealth. As far as industry is concerned, the only sector to have benefited from any significant development is the oil production in Kermanshah province. The construction industry is an essential one, but industries with any technological potential are non-existent. As a result, income levels in Kurdistan are significantly lower than the national average; in 1975, the figures were 150 dollars and 1,340 dollars respectively, although incomes have grown rapidly because of the increase in the price of oil. Because of the lack of industrial development, there are still very few workers in Kurdistan and, since opportunities for employment are scarce, there has been a major exodus towards the richer regions such as Khuzistan, Tehran, Isphahan, etc. In this way, Kurdistan is shedding the most productive part of its population and this is benefiting the already industrialised centres.

As far as health care is concerned, Kurdistan suffers from a lack of personnel. There are proportionally far fewer doctors than in the rest of the country and diseases such as malaria or tuberculosis are endemic.

Because schooling in the Kurdish language is banned in Iran, Kurdish children are taught in Persian. The number of schools does not meet the needs of the population: it is not unusual for a village to have one teacher for 250 or 300 children. Many children do not attend school at all, particularly in the villages. The rate of illiteracy is therefore particularly high: in 1975 more than 70 per cent of the population was illiterate, for women the figure went up to 80 per cent. At that time, two out of five girls and one in four boys of school age did not attend school at all. Virtually all the women in the countryside were illiterate (95 per cent); the figure for men was 85 per cent. In the towns the figures were lower: 60 per cent of women and 40 per cent of men. Kurdish intellectuals generally express themselves and write in Persian because this is the language of the education system. Although the teaching of the Kurdish language is forbidden, there are governmental radio stations, notably in Kermanshah, which broadcast in Kurdish. This contributes to the perpetuation of a living culture. The influence of Iraq, where publications in Kurdish are authorised, has had an effect on the renewal of Kurdish culture.

5. The Kurds in Syria

From tolerance to oppression

There has not been a census of the Kurds in Syria, but their numbers can be estimated at 10 per cent of the population, or close to a million people. Only 1 per cent of the Kurds live in Arab towns, mainly Aleppo, Damascus, which has a real Kurdish neighbourhood, and Hamah. Three regions have a Kurdish majority: Jazira, Kurd Dagh, Jebel Samaan and Aza. These regions are quite distinct, separated by areas populated by Arabs. There is therefore no Syrian Kurdistan. Since the Arab population of the Jazira region has remained nomadic, the Kurds, with the support of the Kurdish population which emigrated from Turkey in the 1920s, have turned these lands into a rich agricultural zone.

More than half of Syria's Kurds live in Jazira. The mainly nomadic Arabic population is concentrated in the southern part of the region. The Kurdish population includes a small number of Yezidis who live near Lake Khatun.

The area around Ain al-Arab, to the north-east of Aleppo, is a totally Kurdish territory with a population of approximately 80,000. Some 350,000 Kurds live in the mountainous area known as Kurd Dagh (the Mountain of the Kurds), to the north-west of Antioch. This dense population remains prosperous thanks to a well-managed form of mountain agriculture.

Historically, the Kurds of Syria were well integrated into society: as Moslems they enjoyed the same rights as the Arabs. In fact it was to a lesser extent the Turkish and Moslem Kurdish military aristocracy which dominated Moslem society in the Middle Ages; and it was the Kurdish Prince Saladin who achieved the decisive victories against the Crusaders in the 12th century.

During the period of the French mandate, the Kurds were able to publish in Syria without hindrance. During the evacuation of Syria by Franco-British troops in 1946, the Arab and Kurdish communities maintained good relations. However, the Arab nationalist movement, which had strong support amongst the Syrian middle-classes, was opposed to any recognition of the rights of the Kurdish minority, although there were no repressive measures taken against it. It was still permitted to publish works of literature in Kurdish. Children received their education in Arabic, but the teaching of Kurdish out of school was not prohibited.

The KDPS (the Kurdish Democratic Party of Syria) was founded in 1957, just before the Ba'ath Party came to power. The Arab nationalist movement, under the influence of the Nasserites, had been pre-eminent in

Damascus since 1956. The intimidation followed by the open oppression of the Kurdish minority began at that time. Records of Kurdish music were smashed in cafés. To publish, or even to possess books written in Kurdish were offences which carried prison sentences.

The KDPS was founded with the help of Jalal Talabani, the Iraqi KDP's representative in Damascus. At that time, the leading figure in the KDPS was Nureddin Zaza. He was born into a middle-class family, in eastern Anatolia, which became dispersed following Shaikh Said's revolt (1925-30). He spent his childhood in Syria and was a pupil at the French Lycée in Damascus. He was imprisoned by the Iraqi authorities in 1944 for having attempted to join General Barzani's troops. After studying at the University of Beirut, he went to Lausanne where he founded the first Kurdish student association. He returned to Damascus in 1956 and, the following year, he laid down the foundations of the KDPS. He was imprisoned and condemned to death for his political activities in 1960 and was only spared as a result of an international campaign. After being freed, a year and a half later he went to the Lebanon and then to Jordan where the government handed him back to the Syrian authorities, who imprisoned him once more. He was finally freed in 1970. He then went into exile in Switzerland where he died of cancer in October 1988.

The movement's other founders, such as the famous poet Osman Sabri, Hamid Hadj Darwish, a law student, or the religious leader Shaikh Muhammad Issa Mahmud also had privileged backgrounds. Nurredin Zaza was the first president of the KDPS. The party's illegal activities at that time consisted of distributing tracts in Arabic and Kurdish, and recruiting activists. The KDPS was opposed to the union of Syria and Egypt, which would confirm the dominance of pro-Arab ideology, and fought against the marginalisation of the Kurds, particularly within the administration.

The party's activities did not remain secret for very long: on 5th August 1960, the secret police arrested and tortured the leaders of Aleppo's executive committee. The KDPS's entire organisation was destroyed, 5,000 people were arrested including Nurredin Zaza, Osman Sabri and Rashid Amo, a teacher and ex-member of the Syrian Communist Party.

In September 1961, the break up of the union with Egypt and the election of a Syrian parliament allowed Shaikh Muhammad Issa Mahmud to be elected as a parliamentary deputy. The election of Nurredin Zaza was invalidated and he finally quit Syria in 1963. From 1961 to 1963, the KDPS was led by Hamid Hadj Darwish who had managed to evade the first wave of arrests in 1960. He was finally captured in 1965 and released ten months later. He was then accused of having collaborated with the government.

In the 1960s, the Kurds, whether or not they belonged to the KDPS, were persecuted by the authorities. A document of the secret police, signed by the man responsible for the province of Jazira, Muhammad Talab Hilal, clearly showed the thinking of certain Arab leaders of that period. Having noted the popularity of the KDPS, Hilal proposed that the region's Kurdish population should be transferred and replaced by an Arab population.

Prior to this study, which was published in 1963, a decree issued on 23rd August 1963 authorised a special census in the province of Jazira to contend with the 'infiltrations' of Kurds from Turkey. Following the results of the census, 120,000 Kurds were deprived of their Syrian citizenship. Without documents, they were unable to marry legally, they could not go to a hospital when they were ill, but they were nevertheless obliged to do military service. Many of them were in fact sent to fight in the Golan Heights in 1967.

In order to launch its arabisation policy, the government set up its plan for an Arab Belt, which provided for the expulsion of the Kurdish population from the area along the border with Turkey, in order to replace it progressively with Arabs. The discovery of oil at Qarachok, in the middle of a Kurdish region, was probably one of the reasons for this policy.

The Ba'ath Party and the Kurds

After the Ba'ath Party assumed power in 1963, the situation of the Kurds took a turn for the worse. The plan for the Arab Belt was not abandoned and the aim of the agricultural reform programme was to expel Kurdish peasants rather than to obtain a better distribution of the land.

Furthermore, the construction of the Tabqa dam made it possible for Arab peasants to settle on Kurdish land. In 1975, 7,000 Arab families were to set up home in this way before Hafiz al-Asad put a stop to the movement.

Faced with this policy of repression, the KDPS was too divided to put up an effective resistance. The party first split in 1965 because of the opposing views held by Osman Sabri and Hamid Hadj Darwish. This crisis mirrored the divisions in the Iraqi KDP: Jalal Talabani, who had studied alongside Hamid Hadj Darwish, was opposed to Barzani, who had Osman Sabri's support.

Despite General Barzani's efforts at reconciliation, the Kurdish movement was split again in 1972 with the founding of a new Kurdish Democratic Party of Syria led by Daham Miro. Daham Miro's party, which was close to Mustafa Barzani, reunited a large number of Kurds who had left the old party because of its divisions. It was thus that Shaikh Muhammad Issa Mahmud and Hamid Sino joined the party. In 1972, with the arrest of its principal leaders, the KDPS's organised activities in Syria were virtually finished.

The Kurds under Hafiz al-Asad's regime

After Hafiz al-Asad came to power in 1972 the condition of the Kurds in Syria began to improve. The Syrian president needed the Kurds for both external and internal reasons. For internal reasons first of all, since the power in Syria was held by a small denominational minority, the Alawites, and it was therefore in Hafiz al-Asad's interest to look after other minorities such as the Kurds. In order to associate the Kurds with the existing government, the regime created Kurdish militias, which were used in the internal repression, led by the Alawis, of the Moslem Brothers in Aleppo in 1980, and in Hama in 1982.

Externally, since the Kurdish minority was small and therefore not a threat to the state, Syria used it to destabilise its neighbours. The dispute between Syria and Turkey had its historic roots in the transfer of the sovereignty of the Sanjak of Alexandretta to Turkey in 1939, under the French Mandate. In addition to this territorial dispute, the present construction of a large dam on the Euphrates (the Atatürk Dam) could deprive Syria of half of its water, and allow Turkey to bring pressures to bear which Syria perceives as threatening. In 1987, an agreement between the two countries included the ending of Damascus's support of the PKK (the closure of the Kurdish movement's bases in Syria) in exchange for guarantees over the supply of water. In practice, the PKK moved its bases from Syria to the Bekaa Valley, under the control of Hafiz al-Asad's government, which refused to extradite Abdullah Ocalan, the PKK's leader, thereby draining the meaning out of the agreement.

The enmity between the two Ba'ath parties in power in Baghdad and Damascus explains the support that the Iraqi Kurds receive from Syria. Syria gives them the chance of diplomatic representation, and is both a sanctuary and an access route into Iraqi Kurdistan.

The relative tolerance of the Syrian authorities does not include granting any rights to its Kurdish minority. Publications in Kurdish and the teaching of the language are prohibited. The government has also banned the festival of *Newroz* (New Year's Day). In 1986, this led to confrontations with the police and a number of people were killed. More recently, in March 1990, a demonstration by Kurds who had been stripped of their nationality in 1962 was put down violently by the police when the demonstrators tried to give a list of their demands to the president of the republic.

This incident happened a few days after the elections that brought about a degree of relaxation of the system. The proportion of seats reserved for the independents in the parliamentary elections rose from 18 per cent to 40 per cent, the rest went to a coalition dominated by the Ba'ath party. Under these circumstances Kurdish voters were able to elect fifteen Kurdish candidates. Three of these stood on the same ticket supported by Syria's Kurdish organisations: Kemal Ahmed, president of the Kurdish Democratic Party of Syria, Hamid Hadj Darwish, president of the Kurdish Progressist Democratic Party of Syria, and Fuad Ekko, a representative of the Kurdish Popular Party. The other successful candidates came from the Kurdish community in Damascus, or some of Syria's other Kurdish regions.

This unusual political success of a minority will reflects the relations that have become established between the leaders of the Kurdish community and the government in office. However, there is always the danger that the Kurds, as the Alawites, will have to pay heavily in the future for the advantages they enjoy today from their association with a particularly repressive government. The reaction of the large *Sunni* majority, should it ever come to power, could provoke a retaliatory period of fierce repression of the Kurds of Syria.

Conclusion

The rights of a minority

In the West, until the appearance of modern nationalism with the French Revolution, and in the Moslem East, at least until the aftermath of the First World War, minorities were only a religious category.

For many of France's Protestants, it was more important to be able to practise their religion in freedom than to remain the subjects of Louis XIV. The Huguenot emigration that followed the revocation of the edict of Nantes in 1685 continued at a good pace until the beginning of the 18th century.

Until the middle of the 19th century, the Ottoman Empire displayed a great deal of tolerance towards its Christian and Jewish religious minorities, which had some autonomy under the *millet* system. As for the Moslems, whatever their origins (Arab, Albanian, Kurdish, etc.), they were a part of the community of believers, the *ummah*.

In Western Europe, it was the middle of the 19th century before the young German and Italian nationalisms took the shape of a unified state. In central and Danubian Europe, most of the states arose later out of the dissolution of the Hapsburg Empire, while some of them were still under Ottoman rule on the eve of the First World War.

The nationalisms in a large part of the Balkans, Caucasia, Asia Minor and the Fertile Crescent, made their first tentative appearances only at the very end of the 19th century. However, everything accelerated rapidly in the aftermath of the First World War. As to rights, the rights of minorities as we understand them today, that is to say ethnic, linguistic as well as religious minorities, were scarcely even mentioned until after the First World War.

Clause 62 of the terms of the Congress of Berlin (1878) stipulated that the Ottoman Empire adhere to the principle of religious freedom.

For the first time, the same Congress of Berlin addressed the problem of minorities from a point of view that was not solely religious. In clause 4 of its terms (which concerned Bulgaria), it was stipulated that in the areas where Bulgarians and Turks, Greeks and Romanians lived together, the rights of these non-Bulgarian minorities had to be taken into account.

These recommendations, however, remained vague. At that time, with the one exception of the right to freedom of religious practice, it was usually protection that was sought for minorities, not rights. However, in practice, in 1878 and 1918, the protection of minorities experienced an overwhelming setback: the Armenian massacres, in 1895-96 under Abdul Hamid, and between 1915 and 1916. While all around a weakened empire nations were running out of patience, it was the minorities which paid the highest price: the deportation of the entire Armenian population of Anatolia and its massacre en route; the deportation and elimination of the Greeks of the Pontus; and the deportations and massacres of the Assyrian Chaldaeans and other Christian minorities from Anatolia.

Even after the First World War, the conceptions concerning minorities remained linked to their religious status. The exchange of populations between Turkey and Greece after the Greek military defeat in 1922 was effected according to religious criteria: 650,000 Moslems were exchanged for 1,200,000 Christians. The fact that many of these Moslems living in Greece spoke Greek rather than Turkish was not taken into account. The reverse was equally true for the Christians.

In the treaty of Lausanne (1923), the clauses concerning minority rights only mentioned non-Moslem religious minorities: Armenians (at least those few tens of thousands that remained), Greeks and Jews had guaranteed rights. But neither the Kurds, as an ethnic and linguistic minority, nor the non-*Sunni* religious minorities — such as the Alawis, for instance — had any rights. The concepts of the period stopped there. It wasn't until 1988 that Richard Schifter, United States assistant secretary of state for human rights and humanitarian affairs, declared that: 'Although they are not mentioned in the Treaty of Lausanne, we believe that the Kurds constitute a national minority according to international law'.[1]

On the international level, the turning point for the rights and the protection of minorities occurred after the First World War. In his fourteen point programme (January 1918), the American president, Woodrow Wilson, set forth — for the benefit of the peoples of Armenia and the Austro-Hungarian Empire — a nation's right to self determination (this did not concern colonised nations). The collapse of the Hapsburg Empire led to the creation of a series of states: Czechoslovakia, Yugoslavia, and Poland. Further to the north, Finland and the three Baltic states became independent. The frontiers of an independent Armenia were set out in the treaty of Sèvres, but were never implemented. The same treaty recognised the Kurds' call for a state on a part of the territories which had a majority Kurdish population.

But the states that were being created in Europe, along the lines of the nation-state, were far from homogenous. After the delineation of the new European frontiers, there appeared in central and Danubian Europe as well as in the Baltic states, nearly 30 million people belonging to minorities. Only 62 per cent of Poles were in Poland, 64 per cent of Czechs and Slovaks in Czechoslovakia, and 70 per cent of Romanians in Romania, while the Ukrainians were divided between three countries.

The League of Nations did not express any internationally valid general definition of the rights of minorities. Instead, it dealt with the problems and the protection of minorities on a case by case basis. Nevertheless, a certain number of general rules were extracted concerning the minorities of Europe (with the exception of the USSR) and those of Iraq after 1923: the right of non-discrimination; access to public office; the right to the use of the native tongue in private as well as in public life; the right to cultural autonomy. In addition, countries were expected to supply the schools and cultural institutions of minorities with material aid.

The League of Nations had the responsibility of attending to the guarantee of these rights; above all it had the legal power, with the permanent international Court of Justice, to settle disputes concerning minorities.

Once again, however, the situation of minorities which were protected, in principle, by the law was to end in tragedy. In 1924, Poland set aside the clauses of the peace treaty concerning minorities. In Turkey, also in 1924, the use of the Kurdish language was banned, as well as all cultural rights. Furthermore, in what is probably the only case of its kind in the annals of the 20th century, the very existence of a Kurdish identity was denied. This anomaly didn't come to an end until 1991.

The suppression of all rights and the strict republicanism of the regime were the cause of three insurrections (in 1925, 1930, and 1936-37) during which the Kurds experienced periods of exceptionally harsh repression as well as mass deportations. The Kurdish regions remained closed to foreigners until 1965, and for three or four decades, Turkey bled its Kurds dry.

In Iraq, the Kurds, who constituted the majority (58 per cent) of the population of the *vilayet* of Mosul, which was incorporated into Iraq by Britain following the First World War because of the oil, were not consulted at all about their wishes for their future status.

The protection of minorities guaranteed by the League of Nations quickly came up against the principle of state sovereignty, and in the end was dependent on the good will of each state.

During the period between the two World Wars, Hitler's Germany was the cause of most minority problems (the Sudeten Germans, etc.). Elsewhere, in Romania, Hungary and Poland, virulent anti-Semitism was used as a lever by ultra nationalist or fascist governments or movements.

Approximately 5 million Jews and several hundred thousand gypsies were exterminated by the Nazis. And, just after Hitler's defeat, there was a huge migratory movement which resulted in the expulsion of some 13 million Germans towards West Germany. They came from the Soviet Union, Poland, Czechoslovakia, the Baltic states and other European countries whose borders had been rectified.

The period following the Second World War was not a propitious one for pro-minority legislation. The crises provoked by Hitler's Germany over the Germanic minorities, particularly the Sudeten Germans, remained fresh in everyone's memory. Human rights, that is to say those of the individual, were considered to be a universal guarantee. If human rights were respected then, it followed by implication that those of an individual belonging to a minority would also be respected.

In addition, the problems of minorities (ethnic, linguistic or religious) were covered by a number of provisions under international law which no organisation had managed to enforce, because they were always problems that concerned the internal affairs of a state, and thus its sovereignty.

In any case, the central concern following the Second World War, apart from the East-West conflict, was the emancipation of the colonial territories of Africa and Asia. Following the First World War, a nation's right to self determination was a European prerogative; following the Second World War it was the prerogative of those countries or peoples that had been colonised by Europeans. 1947 to 1962 was the most active period for decolonisation. The problems linked to minority questions soon began to reappear and, from then on, never left the centre of the international stage: the Kurds of Iraq (from 1961); southern Sudan; Eritrea (from 1962); Tibet; the Tamils of Sri Lanka; the Sikhs, etc.

Problems of oppressed or discriminated against minorities also appeared in the Danubian and Balkan parts of Europe: the Hungarians of Transylvania (Romania), the Albanians of Kosovo (Yugoslavia), the Turks of Bulgaria, etc. Similar problems also surfaced in the Soviet Union, particularly with the Crimean Tartars, the Meskhs of Uzbekistan and the Armenians of Karabagh.

It was in 1966 that the General Assembly of the United Nations stipulated in article 27 of its International Covenant on Civil and Political Rights: 'In those countries in which ethnic, religious and linguistic minorities exist, persons belonging to such minorities shall not be denied the right in community with other members of their group, to enjoy their own culture, to profess and practise their own religion or to use their own language.'

The provisions of article 27 were considered to be the minimal expression of the rights of a minority: cultural rights and the right to an identity. Nonetheless, there is undeniable evidence of the oppression and discrimination of minorities (and sometimes of majorities) in a great many non-democratic countries. The fate of a minority continues to depend exclusively on the good-will of a country (or on its level of democracy). In half a century, the International Court of Justice has never investigated a minority problem.

In 1975, the final act of the Helsinki Agreement raised a number of points concerning the problems and the protection of minorities.

Nevertheless, wherever there is no democracy, or whenever it comes to an end, the discrimination and the cultural or physical oppression of minorities continue to exist without any sign of improvement.

In June 1989, the Conference on Security and Co-operation in Europe (CSCE) published a charter for the rights of ethnic minorities. This charter was a major step forward in international law.[2]

The United Nations is also seeking to establish something more than a minimum in so far as minority rights are concerned (cf. Appendix 2). But the heart of the problem lies not only in the rights accorded to minorities under international law, but also in the procedures through which the law can at least be defended, even if it can't be guaranteed. What political or moral measures could be taken against a state which might break, in a flagrant manner, the internationally recognised rights of a minority? This is undoubtedly the question which needs to be addressed if we are not to be condemned merely to deplore such violations, and counting the victims. Is it more legitimate to discriminate against, to oppress and to crush a minority than to be a state founded on apartheid? If there was incontestable proof that a country had broken the rules concerning minorities which it had agreed to abide by when it became a member of the United Nations, why shouldn't the other member states take the same sort of action as they have against South Africa and boycott it? Following the Cold War, it is now time to consider a new advance in so far as the rights of minorities are concerned. But this must not be limited to declarations. Sanctions and concrete measures will be required if further long, harsh conflicts are to be avoided in the future.

Notes

1. Cited by M.M. Gunter, *op cit.*, p. 117.

2. Cf. Alain Fenet, 'La question des minorités dans l'ordre du droit', in *Les Minorités à l'âge de l'État-nation, Groupement pour les droits des minorités*, G.Chaliand (éd.), Fayard, 1985.

Appendix 1: Resolution 688

Adopted by the Security Council of the United Nations

The Security Council,

Mindful of its duties and its responsibilities under the Charter of the United Nations for the maintenance of international peace and security,

Recalling Article 2, paragraph 7, of the Charter of the United Nations,[1]

Gravely concerned by the repression of the Iraqi civilian population in many parts of Iraq, including most recently in Kurdish populated areas which led to a massive flow of refugees towards and across international frontiers and to cross border incursions, which threaten international peace and security in the region,

Deeply disturbed by the magnitude of the human suffering involved,

Taking note of the letters sent by the representatives of Turkey and France to the United Nations dated 2 April 1991 and 4 April 1991, respectively,

Taking note also of the letters sent by the permanent representative of the Islamic republic of Iran to the United Nations dated 3 and 4 April 1991, respectively,

Reaffirming the commitment of all member states to the sovereignty, territorial integrity and political independence of Iraq and of all states in the area,

Bearing in mind the secretary-general's report of 20 March 1991,[2]

1. Condemns the repression of the Iraqi civilian population in many parts of Iraq, including most recently in Kurdish populated areas, the consequences of which threaten international peace and security in the region;

2. Demands that Iraq, as a contribution to removing the threat to international peace and security in the region, immediately end this repression and express the hope in the same context that an open dialogue will take place to ensure that the human and political rights of all Iraqi citizens are respected;

3. Insists that Iraq allow immediate access by international humanitarian organisation to all those in need of assistance in all parts of Iraq and to make available all necessary facilities for their operations;

4. Requests the secretary-general to pursue his humanitarian efforts in Iraq and to report forthwith, if appropriate on the basis of a further mission to the region, on the plight of the Iraqi civilian population, and in particular the Kurdish population, suffering from the repression in all its forms inflicted by the Iraqi authorities;

5. Requests further the secretary-general to use all the resources at his disposal, including those of the relevant United Nations agencies, to address urgently the critical needs of the refugees and displaced Iraqi population;

6. Appeals to all member states and to all humanitarian organisations to contribute to these humanitarian relief efforts;

7. Demands that Iraq co-operate with the secretary-general to these ends;

8. Decides to remain seized of the matter.

Notes

1. Which stipulates that the United Nations are not authorised to intervene in the affairs which relate to the national competence of states. (n. d. a.).

2. The report by Matti Athisaari on the humanitarian situation in Iraq (n. d. a.)

Appendix 2: Resolution adopted by the European Parliament

Joint motion for resolution tabled by

-Mrs Dury, on behalf of the Socialist Group,

Mr Penders and Mrs Cassanmagnago Cerretti, on behalf of the Group of the European People's Party,

Mr Bertens and Mr Calvo Ortega, on behalf of the Liberal and Democratic Reformist Group,

Mr Christopher Jackson and Mr McMillan-Scott, on behalf of the European Democratic Group,

Mrs Roth and Mr Langer, on behalf of the Green Group,

Mr Colajanni, on behalf of the Group for the European United Left,

Mr de la Malène, on behalf of the Group of the European Democratic Alliance,

Mr Vandemeulebroucke and Mrs Ewing, on behalf of the Rainbow Group,

Mr Piquet, on behalf of Left Unity ....

On the situation of the Kurds

Motion adopted unanimously.

The European Parliament,

Having regard to the relevant resolutions of the UN Security Council,

Having regard to its previous resolutions on the situation of the Kurds,

Having regard to the results of the European Council of 8 April 1991 in Luxembourg,

A. Whereas the forces under the command of Saddam Hussein are attempting to commit genocide against the Kurds,

B. Having regard to the general acts of tyranny including the widespread use of torture committed by Saddam Hussein and his forces against the population, including children, in Iraq,

C. Whereas thousands of people are dying from the effects of bombing attacks and the bombing of Kurdish areas is continuing,

D. Profoundly shocked at the terrible suffering experienced by thousands of Kurdish refugees fleeing across mountainous regions, without shelter and in absolute destitution, and alarmed at the dramatic news from humanitarian organisations on the spot, according to which thousands of refugees, predominantly children, have died on the road from hunger, cold, disease and the consequences of their wounds, and that, according to doctors, hundreds more are dying every day,

E. Emphasising that the Iraqi army is carrying out executions among the *Shi'ite* population in the south of the country,

F. Whereas members of the coalition led the Iraqi opposition to believe that moves to oust Saddam Hussein would be welcomed and supported,

G. Aware that, until a political solution is found to the Kurdish problem, it will continue to pose a threat to peace and security in the region,

1. Strongly condemns the attempted genocide against the Kurds by Saddam Hussein's regime and the repression of the Iraqi population as a whole;

2. Calls for an immediate end to attacks on the population and reaffirms the need to maintain in full the United Nations embargo as long as acts of repression against the Kurdish people and the Iraqi population as a whole continue;

3. Supports the proposal submitted at the European Council for the creation of temporary protected zones to ensure the safety of Kurds and other displaced persons in Iraq, but is concerned at the consequences of prolonging this situation; supports the decision already taken to provide aid for the Kurds and urges that this aid be adequate and effective; consequently welcomes the decision of the US, British and French governments to send troops to Iraq to guarantee the security of these zones;

4. Calls on the governments of Iran and Turkey to facilitate the supply of aid to the Kurdish populations and to open their national frontiers to refugees and international non-governmental humanitarian organisations; calls on the international community, under the auspices of the United Nations, to support efforts being made to this end;

5. Emphasises the moral duty of the United Nations, if necessary by amending the UN charter, to go beyond the mere preservation of national boundaries and to develop means of preventing totalitarian regimes from perpetrating genocide;

6. Notes that the treatment of the Kurdish people is tantamount to the crime of genocide within the meaning of the 1948 Convention, as noted by the Foreign Ministers meeting European Political Co-operation; calls on the governments of the Member states to bring the matter before the International Court of Justice to ensure that these acts of genocide are acknowledged and condemned in accordance with that Convention;

7. Hopes that the Kurdish problem can be placed on the agenda of a Middle East peace conference with the participation of all the states concerned together with Kurdish representatives to secure recognition of the Kurds' right to existence and autonomy in all countries in which they are to be found;

8. Welcomes Resolution 688 of the UN Security Council on the situation of the Kurds in Iraq and hopes that the Security Council will take all necessary measures to guarantee the security of the Kurdish population and enable Kurdish refugees to return to their homes with the guarantee that they will not be the victims of any form of persecution;

9. Insists that no-one fleeing from the Iraqi regime must be forced to return to Iraq against their will and calls on the Member states of the Community to facilitate arrangements for Kurdish refugees requesting asylum;

10. Considers that the enforcement of Resolution 688 will require the presence of an adequate United Nations peace-keeping force;

11. Instructs the Enlarged Bureau to consider sending a parliamentary delegation to the region;

12. Instructs its president to forward this resolution to the Council, the Commission, the United Nations and the governments of Turkey, Iran, Syria and Iraq.

Appendix 3: Villages Bombarded with Chemical Weapons by the Iraqi Airforce

As drawn up by the Kurdish Institute in Paris

Date	Villages	Casualties
15 April 1987	Haladin, Bargalo,Kanito, Awazic, Sirwan, Noljika, Chinara (Sulaymaniya province)	Dozens of dead and wounded
16 April 1987	Sheikwasan, Totma, Zeni, Khati, Balalokawa, Alana, Daresh (Balasan valley, Arbil province) 286 wounded trying to get to Arbil for medical attention, were all captured and killed by the Iraqi army	121 dead, of whom 76 were children aged from 1 day to 8 years, at Sheikwasan
17 April 1987	Qizlar, Singar, Mijokala (Sulaymaniya province)	10 dead
18 April 1987	Regions around Qaywan	2 dead
19 April 1987	Moutain, Kovak, Konakotr	52 wounded
19 April 1987	Balasan valley	
21 April 1987	Karadagh region (Sulaymaniya province)	hundreds of wounded
1 May 1987	Ziywi (Dohuk region)	2 dead and some wounded
23 May 1987	Tomar, Gargan, Qamargan, near Kirkuk	10 dead, 7 of whom were children
27 May 1987	Nalahan, Gorascher, Kandola	47 children killed

	Bardok, Bily, Nali, Tahi	74 dead, hundreds wounded
27 June 1987	Balaran valley	dozens dead
	Ziywi and Peramagron	35 wounded
	Saragalo, Bargalo, Yakhsamar, Haladin, Naloma	5 women and children dead, dozens wounded
3 Sept 1987	Bargalo, Yakhsamar	4 dead
14 Sept 1987	Mearga Pan	41 wounded
25 Feb 1988	Saregalo, Yakhsamar, Haladin, Gayzla, Jaffty valley	63 dead, 800 wounded
16 March 1988	Halabja, Inab, Zamagri	5,000 dead, 9,000 wounded
22 March 1988	Shanakhsi region	10 dead, 460 wounded
	Siwsiman, Dokan, Balakajar, Jafaran, Walean, Karadagh region (Sulaymaniya province)	75 dead, of whom 47 women and children, over 300 wounded
27 March 1988	412 wounded coming from Karadagh seeking help in Sulaymaniya	
14 April 1988	Garmian region	dozens of dead
15 April 1988		
16 April 1988		

		dozens of wounded
23 April 1988		
25 April 1988		
26 April 1988		
27 April 1988		
3 May 1988	Goptapa, Askar, Garchinan, Galnagaj, Sotka, Kalashera, Zarzy, Koya region, Chaimrezan	112 dead, 844 wounded
15 May 1988	Nazaneen, Hiran, Doli, Simakloy, Wari	51 dead, hundreds wounded

Appendix 4: Chronology

7th century Converted to Islam, the Kurds contribution to Moslem civilisation is particularly noteworthy in the military and musical spheres. A Kurdish musician from Mosul, Ibrahim Mawsili (743-806), sets up the first scholarly Moslem academy of music at the court of Harun al Rashid, which his son Ishaq develops and codifies in Baghdad.

10th-12th centuries The emergence of the independent Kurdish principalities: in the north, the Shaddadides (951-1174), capital Ganja; in the south, the Hassawaihides (959-1015); in the west, the Marwanids (990-1174), capital Diyarbakir.

1169-1250 The Ayyubid dynasty rules over the Moslem Middle-East. Saladin is its most illustrious representative.

14th-15th centuries The restoration of the Kurdish principalities following the upheavals of the Mongol invasion. Kurdish cultural life blossoms at the courts of Bitlis, Hakiâri and Botan.

1514 The alliance of the Kurdish princes with the Ottoman Sultan Selim 'the grim' against *Shi'ite* Persia. The Shah's army is beaten by Turco-Kurdish forces at Chaldiran (in the north of Kurdistan). Autonomous Kurdish principalities make up the Empire's eastern borders.

1596 Sharaf Khan, mir of Bitlis, completes his *Sharafname* (Annals of the Turkish Peoples), the first history of the Kurds.

1695 Ahmad-i Khani produces his masterwork, the Kurdish national epic poem *Mem u Zin*, in which he calls for the establishment of a unified Kurdish state.

19th century The Sublime Porte carries out its policy of centralisation. Their privileges under threat, the Kurdish Princes rise up in extended order: 1806, the revolt of Abdurrahman Pasha of Sulaymaniya; 1818, the Bibas uprising; 1832, the revolt of Bedr Khan Beg; 1853-55, the revolt of Yezdan Sher; 1880, the revolt of Shaikh Ubaydallah of Nehri.

1898 The appearance of the first Kurdish newspaper: *Kurdistan*.

1908 The Young Turk revolution. The proclamation in Constantinople of a Constitution promulgating the equality of all the nationalities in the empire. But, from 1909, the Young Turks adopt a policy of ultra nationalism. Kurdish associations and publications are banned.

30th October 1918 The Mudros Armistice. Having made common cause with Germany during the Great War, the defeated Ottoman Empire surrenders to the Allies.

19-26th April 1920 The San Remo Conference. The many agreements concluded by the Allies during the course of the war, concerning the division of the Middle East, are brought up to date in the light of the new balance of powers. Great Britain is given the mandate for Arabian Iraq and the Kurdish *vilayet* of Mosul, France the mandate for Syria.

1919-1920 The first Kurdish revolt in the *vilayet* of Mosul, led by Shaikh Mahmud, is put down by the British, by means of the RAF.

10th August 1920 The Allies and the Sublime Porte conclude the treaty of Sèvres which confirms the divisions established in San Remo. In section III (art. 62-64), the treaty advocates the creation of a Kurdish state.

23rd August 1921 After having been ousted from Syria by the French, Mir Faisal, the son of the *Sharif* of Mecca is enthroned as King of Iraq by Sir Percy Cox, the British high commissioner in Mesapotamia. There is a mass boycott by the Kurds of Mosul of the plebiscite organised for the election of Faisal.

20th October 1921 The Franco-Turkish Ankara agreement. France annexes the two Kurdish provinces of Jazira and Kurd-Dagh to Syria which had been placed under its mandate.

1922-1923 Shaikh Mahmud's second revolt. He proclaims himself 'King of Kurdistan' and enters into contact with the Iranian Kurdish leader Simko who has been rebelling against Persian rule since 1920. The movement is put down by the British and the Shaikh is exiled.

24th June 1923 Ankara's Kemalist government and the Allied Powers sign the treaty of Lausanne which supersedes the treaty of Sèvres.

3rd March 1924 In Turkey a decreed law bans all Kurdish schools, associations and publications for the same reason as the religious brotherhoods and the madrasa. The first Turkish Assembly, which includes 72 representatives from Kurdistan, is dissolved.

February-April 1925 Shaikh Said's revolt in Turkish Kurdistan. The first deportations of Kurdish populations.

16th December 1925 The Council of the League of Nations accedes to the British demand to annexe the *vilayet* of Mosul to the state of Iraq.

August 1927 The founding congress of *Hoybun* (Independence); the National Kurdish League. This organisation unites all the Kurdish political circles, groups and parties created after the Great War.

1928 The entire civil and military administration of Turkey's Kurdish provinces is placed under the control of the Turkish high commissioner for these regions.

1930 There is a growing rebel movement, under the leadership of *Hoybun*, in the Mount Ararat region. Turkey and Iran come to terms in order to quell it.

June 1930 Simko, the Iranian Kurdish leader who has been in rebellion against the government since 1920, is assassinated during the course of negotiations with representatives from Tehran.

Autumn 1931 Jafar Sultan leads a new revolt in Iranian Kurdistan.

1931 Shaikh Mahmud returns from exile and once more raises the banner of rebellion in Iraqi Kurdistan. He is taken prisoner by the British and put under house arrest in Baghdad. Soon after, the Iraqi Kurds rise up, this time under the leadership of Shaikh Ahmad Barzani, Mustafa Barzani's brother. The British RAF intervenes to crush the rebellion.

May 1932 Ankara passes a law which legalises the deportation and dispersion of the Kurds. There are mass deportations to central Anatolia.

1933 The Barzanis lead a new revolt in Iraq.

1936-1938 Very harsh measures are used to subdue the great uprising in Dersim (Turkey). Turkey's Kurdish rebel movements are bled dry.

1943-1945 Mustafa Barzani leads a revolt in Iraq before escaping to Iranian Kurdistan with his followers.

August 1945 The Iranian KDP is founded and, soon after, a similar organisation is set up by the Kurds in Iraq.

13th January 1946 At the instigation of the Soviet Union, the first Kurdish republic is proclaimed at Mahabad. It is presided over by Qazi Muhammad. It is crushed less than a year later. Barzani, the leader of the Kurdish forces, and a few hundred of his followers manage to beat a retreat across the Turkish-Iranian borders and find refuge in the USSR.

August 1953 The Shah of Iran is returned to power by a *coup d'état* organised by the CIA.

1956 Under the aegis of Great Britain and the United States, Turkey, Iran and Iraq sign the Baghdad pact. One of the pact's clauses provides for the co-ordinated repression of any revolt that might break out on the territory of one of the three states. It finds an immediate application when the Kurdish uprising in the province of Jouanroj (Iran) is put down by combined Iraqi and Iranian forces.

1957 The Syrian KDP is established and banned.

14th July 1958 Iraq's Hashemite monarchy is overthrown by a military *coup d'état* led by General Qasim. The Republic in which 'Arabs and Kurds are freely associated' is proclaimed in Baghdad. Barzani returns from exile in the Soviet Union.

9th January 1960 The Iraqi KDP is legalised.

27th May 1960 In Turkey, the Menderes government is overthrown by a military *coup d'état*. The military convoke a constituent assembly which draws up a new Turkish Constitution, more liberal than the previous ones.

Spring 1961 In Iraq, Kurdish journals and publications are charged with 'separatism' and gradually banned.

11th September 1961 The start of the Kurdish armed insurrection in Iraq.

8th February 1963 The Ba'athist *coup d'état* in Baghdad. A provisional cease-fire on the Kurdistan front. A communist witch hunt in which several thousand are imprisoned or killed. The survivors find refuge with the Kurdish underground forces.

June 1963 The Iraqi army unleashes a new offensive against the Kurdish underground. Syria, where the Ba'ath Party had come to power following its March 1963 *coup d'état*, sends its army and air force to participate in the fight against the Kurds.

18th November 1963 In Baghdad, General Aref ousts the Ba'athists from power and acquires the rank of marshal.

10th February 1964 After Marshall Aref declares his recognition of the national rights of the Kurds, a cease-fire is agreed. The political expediency of this agreement divides the Kurdish leadership. Ibrahim Ahmed and Jalal Talabani, who run the political wing of the KDP, are opposed to General Barzani, the movement's leader. The disagreements soon degenerate into armed clashes. The political wing seeks refuge in Iran, before returning to Baghdad in order to join up with the regime. There is an atmosphere of crisis and confusion in the ranks of the Iraqi Kurdish movement.

March 1965 The resumption of military actions which will be continued until the cease-fire of June 1966.

Autumn 1965 Having been declared 'a military zone prohibited to foreigners' in 1925, Turkey's Kurdish provinces are now open to foreign visitors.

1967-1968 A peasant guerilla campaign in Iranian Kurdistan.

July 1968 In Baghdad, the Ba'ath Party is back in power following two successive *coups d'état* (19th and 30th July). General al-Bakr, Prime Minister of the Ba'athist government of 1963, is proclaimed president of the republic. The war against Barzani's fighters starts up again in April 1963.

11th March 1970 An Iraqi-Kurdish agreement on the autonomy of Kurdistan, its institutions to be in place within a four year period.

1970-1974 A period of 'neither war nor peace' in Iraqi Kurdistan. The government-inspired attempts on the lives of Kurdish leaders, the policy for the arabisation of Kurdish border lands and the differences over the territorial basis of the autonomous region, have a damaging effect on the relations between the Kurdish movement and the government in Baghdad.

12th March 1971 Military coup in Turkey. Left wing parties and organisations are banned. Several thousand Kurdish 'separatists' are arrested and tried by military tribunals. A parliamentary regime is reinstated in October 1973.

Spring 1972 Reversal of alliances. As a part of its internal and external strategy for the isolation of the Kurdish movement, the Iraqi regime concludes a friendship and co-operation treaty with the USSR which, up until then, had supported the Kurds. Iran decides to back the Kurds, with Washington's discreet support.

March 1974 Baghdad issues a 'Kurdish Autonomy Law', a watered down version of the 1970 agreement, and calls upon the Kurdish leadership to rubber stamp it. By April, the war has started up again on a greater scale than ever before.

5th March 1975 The Algiers agreement between the Shah of Iran and the Iraqi vice Premier, Saddam Hussein. Iran decides to cease giving military support to the Iraqi Kurds.

End of March 1975 The Kurdish leadership abandons the struggle and takes refuge in Iran. The Kurdish resistance collapses.

June 1976 Renewed guerilla activity in Iraqi Kurdistan.

1977-1978 The upsurge of the Kurdish movements in Turkey. The founding of the PKK.

February 1979 The overthrow of the monarchy in Iran. The Kurdish national movement, led by A. R. Ghassemlou, controls Mahabad.

March 1979 Mustafa Barzani dies in the United States. The Iranian government authorises his burial in Iran.

August 1979 Ayatollah Khomeini declares a *jihad*, a 'holy war' against the Kurds of Iran. Dozens of Kurdish activists are executed without trial. For the Kurds of Iran, this is the beginning of a prolonged period of armed struggle.

September 1980 A military *coup d'état* in Turkey. Repression of the Kurds (amongst others).

September 1980 The beginning of the Iran-Iraq war. Iraq denounces the Algiers agreement and launches a huge offensive against Iran. The internal conflicts between the Iranian Kurds and the government in Tehran, and the Iraqi Kurds and the government in Baghdad are used, as much by Iran as by Iraq, to weaken the rival state, while the various Kurdish movements are attempting to strengthen themselves.

May-June 1983 With the agreement of Baghdad, Turkish special forces enter Iraqi Kurdistan for a cleaning up operation in the border areas where the PKK has its refuge.

July 1983 The Iraqi army surrounds the important villages of Qoshtapa and Diyala in the province of Arbil, where a large number of Barzani's followers had been forced to live after their defeat in 1975. All males between the ages of 12 and 70 were arrested and transferred to an unknown destination. The fate of these men, believed to be some 8,000 in number, remains unknown.

October 1983 There are violent clashes between Iraq and Iran resulting in several thousand deaths amongst the Kurdish populations in the regions of Penjwin and Garmak. Mehdi Zana, the former elected mayor of the town of Diyarbakir, is condemned to 25 years imprisonment. During the same trial, over a hundred members of the Turkish KSP received sentences of between 6 months and 19 years imprisonment.

December 1983 Jalal Talabani enters into negotiations with the Iraqi government. These last for a year before being suspended by Baghdad. The war is resumed.

January 1984 The prisoners in Diyarbakir military prison begin a hunger strike as a protest against torture. six Kurdish prisoners die during the course of the month, eleven others die at the beginning of March as a result of hunger strikes.

June 1984 Between 200 and 300 people are killed during Iraqi raids on the town of Baneh in Iranian Kurdistan.

1984 The beginning of the PKK's guerilla operations in Turkey.

February 1985 During the course of a trial which, because of the number of defendants, is one of the most important in the history of the Turkish republic, 22 members of the PKK are condemned to death and 301 others to sentences of between 3 years and life imprisonment. All of them were accused of having attempted to set up 'an independent Marxist-Leninist state on a part of Turkey's territory'.

April 1985 The alliance, sealed in 1981 between Masud Rajavi's People's Mujahidin and the Iranian KDP led by A.R. Ghassemlou, is officially broken.

November 1985 According to Amnesty International, a large number of Kurdish prisoners were executed in Abu-Guraib, 60 or so during the first week of the month and at least as many in the prison at Mosul (Iraq). On the 15th November, the Turkish air force bombed *peshmerga* positions in the Iraqi provinces of Arbil and Zakho. Turkish ground forces also entered into the Zakho region of Iraq.

January 1987 Idris Barzani, one of the main leaders of the Iranian KDP, dies at the age of 43. The mutilated bodies of 29 Kurdish adolescents, arrested in September-October 1985 in Iraq, are returned to their families in exchange for the payment of a sum of money for 'execution expenses'.

February 1987 According to the Turkish daily newspaper *Cumhuriyet*, a total of 240 books have been seized in Turkey since 1983 for 'separatist propaganda and attacks on national unity'. These include *Map of the World* and *Map of Europe and the World*, published by Penguin.

March 1987 In its annual report on world human rights violations, the American State Department mentioned the case of the Kurds of Turkey for the first time. According to the Turkish daily *Cumhuriyet*, the publication of this report caused 'serious embarrassment' in Ankara.

April 1987 The European Parliament adopts a resolution condemning the torturing to death of Kurdish adolescents in Iraq.

15th-22nd April 1987 Iraq uses chemical weapons and mustard gas against the Kurdish population in Iraq. At least 20 villages are affected and approximately 500 people killed.

June 1987 In its resolution of the 18th June, the European Parliament recognises the genocide of the Armenians and calls on Turkey to recognise the existence of its Kurdish minority.

August 1987 The Iraqi air force drops chemical weapons on Kardasht where some of the Iraqi Kurdish refugees are gathered.

1987 The creation of the Iraqi Kurdistan Front, a coalition of eight organisations.

March 1988 5,000 people are killed when the town of Halabja (Iraq) is bombed with chemical weapons.

May 1988 According to the tally drawn up by Kurdish organisations, of the 5,086 villages in Iraqi Kurdistan in 1975, 3,479 had been destroyed.

20th August 1988 Cease-fire agreement between Iraq and Iran.

25th August-10th September 1988 Iraqi chemical weapon offensive against the northern provinces along the Turkish frontier: 100,000 Kurds seek refuge in Turkey. Two thirds of them are sent to Iran, the others are installed in camps 'on a temporary basis' by the Turkish authorities.

13th July 1989 Abdul Rahman Ghassemlou, the Secretary General of the Iranian KDP, is assassinated in Vienna during negotiations with Iranian emissaries. According to the Turkish authorities 'in 1989, 136 civilians and 153 members of the security forces were killed in acts of terrorism, sometimes instigated from bases abroad'.

10th May 1990 The publication of legal decrees 84 and 85, which give the regional governor of the south-eastern provinces of Turkey (Elazig, Bingöl, Tunceli, Van, Diyarbakir, Mardin, Siirt, Hakkari, Barman, Sirnak) considerable repressive powers for an indefinite period.

August 1990 The annexation of Kuwait by Iraq.

17th January 1991 The Gulf War which ends on 6th March.

March 1991 Following the *Shi'ite* insurrection in the south of Iraq, the Kurdish population rises in rebellion. Between 6th and 14th March, the Kurds take control of virtually all the Kurdish towns. Turkey authorises the speaking of Kurdish in public, banned since 1985.

14th-18th March 1991 The battle for Kirkuk is won by the *peshmergas*.

27th March 1991 The counter offensive of Saddam Hussein's elite troops provokes a huge exodus of some 1.5 million people, with the majority fleeing towards Iran and a further 600,000 towards Turkey.

5th April 1991 The Security Council of the UN adopts resolution 688 which condemns the repression of the Iraqi civilian population.

10th April 1991 Washington bans Baghdad from using its air force in the north of Iraq.

16th April 1991 The United States accepts the European idea for an intervention by ground forces onto Iraqi territory in order to protect the

Kurdish refugees. A few days later, American, British and French troops arrive in the Zakho area.

24th April 1991 Saddam Hussein and the Kurdish front announce an agreement in principle which would formalise the autonomy of Kurdistan. This agreement, born of necessity, leads to lengthy negotiations.

May 1991 12,000 American, British and French soldiers are deployed in the allied security zone (there are a further 21,700 in Turkey).

24th June 1991 The number of allied troops is reduced to 5,100 (and 11,000 in Turkey).

August 1991 Turkish forces go into northern Iraq for several days on a mopping-up operation.

November 1991 Iraqi bombardments result in a further 200,000 Kurdish refugees.

December 1991 Mr. Demirel, the new leader of the Turkish government, recognises 'the Kurdish reality'.

May 1992 Kurdish elections held in Iraqi Kurdistan.

Appendix 5: Bibliography

Arfa, Hassan, *The Kurds: An Historical and Political Study*, London, Oxford University Press, 1966.

Barchard, David, *Turkey and the West*, London, Routledge & Kegan Paul for the Royal Institute of International Affairs, 1985.

Berberoglu, Berch, *Turkey in Crisis*, London, Zed Press, 1982.

Besikçi, Ismaïl, *Dogu Anadolu'nun Düzeni: Sosyo-Ekonomik ve Etnik Temeler (The Order of Eastern Anatolia, Socio-Economic and Ethnic Foundations)*, Istanbul, E. Yayinlari, 1970.

Birand, Mehmet Ali, *The General's Coup in Turkey: An Inside Story of 12 September 1980*, M.A. Dikerdem (trans.), London, Brassey's Defence Publishers, 1987.

Bois, Thomas, The Kurds, M.W.M Welland (trans.), Beirut, Khayats, 1965.

Chaliand, Gérard (ed.), *People Without a Country: The Kurds and Kurdistan*, London, Zed Books, 1980.

Driver, G.R., *Kurdistan and the Kurds*, Mount Carmel, GSI Printing Section, 1919.

Eagleton, William, Jr, *The Kurdish Republic of 1946*, London, Oxford University Press, 1963.

Eagleton, William, Jr, *La République kurde*, Bruxelles, Complexe, 1991.

Edmonds, C.J., *Kurds, Turks and Arabs: Politics, Travel and Research in North-Eastern Iraq, 1919-1925*, London, Oxford University Press, 1957.

Ghareeb, Edmund, *The Kurdish Question in Iraq*, Syracuse, Syracuse University Press, 1981.

Ghassemlou, Abdul Rahman, *Kurdistan and The Kurds*, Prague, Czechoslovakian Academy of Science.

Gunter, Michael M., *The Kurds in Turkey: A Political Dilemma*, Wesport, Greenwood Press, 1991.

Hale, Wikkiam M. (ed.), *Aspects of Modern Turkey*, London, Bowker, 1976.

Hale, Wikkiam M. (ed.), *The Political and Economic Development of Modern Turkey*, New York, St. Martin's Press, 1981.

Harris, George, *Turkey: Coping with Crisis*, Boulder, Westview Press, 1970.

Heyd, Uriel, *The Foundations of Turkish Nationalism: The Life and Teachings of Ziya Gökalp*. London, Harvil Press, 1950.

Jafar, Majeed R., *Under-Development: A Regional Case Study of the Kurdish Area in Turkey*, Helsinki, Social Policy Association, 1976.

Jawad, Sa'ad, *Irak and the Kurdish Question, 1958-1970*, London, Ithaca Press, 1981.

Kahn, Margaret, *Children of the Jinn. In Search of the Kurds and their Country*, New York, Seaview Books, 1980.

Kinnane, Derek, *The Kurds and Kurdistan*, London, Oxford University Press, 1964.

Kutschera, Chris, *Le Mouvement national kurde*, Paris, Flammarion, 1979.

Landau, Jacob M., *The Emergence of Modern Turkey*, Leyde, E.J. Brill, 1974.

More, Christiane, *Les Kurdes aujourd'hui: mouvement national et parti politique*, Paris, L'Harmattan, 1984.

O'Ballance, Edgar, *The Kurdish Revolt: 1961-1970*, Hamden, Archon Books, 1973.

Olson, Robert, *The Emergence of Kurdish Nationalism and the Sheikh Said Rebellion, 1880-1925*, Austin, University of Texas Press, 1989.

Ozdubun, Ergun, *The Role of the Military in Recent Turkish Politics*, Cambridge, Harvard University, Center for International Affairs, 1966.

Pelletiere, Stephen, *The Kurds: an Unstable Element in the Gulf*, Boulder, Westview Press, 1984.

Pevsner, Lucille, *Turkey's Political Crisis: Background, Perspectives, Prospects*, New York, Praeger, 1984.

Picard, Elisabeth (ed.), *La Question kurde*, Brussels, Complexe, 1991.

Poppenburg, Walter, *Bücher uber die Kurden und Kurdistan: Eine auswahlt Bibliographie*, Bonn, Verlag fur Kultur und Wissenschaft, 1987.

Rambout, L., *Les Kurdes et le Droit*, Paris, Éditions du Cerf, 1947.

Rustow, Dankwart A., *Turkey: America's Forgotten Ally*, New York, Holt, Rinehart & Winston, 1983.

Short, Martin, McDermott, Anthony, *The Kurds*, London, Minority Rights Group, 1975 and 1987.

Tamkoc, Metin, *The Warrior Diplomats: Guardians of National Security and the Modernisation of Turkey*, Salt Lake City, University of Utah Press, 1976.

Van Bruinessen, M., *Agha, Sheikh and State: The Social and Political Structures of Kurdistan*, London, Zed Books, 1992.

Vanly, Ismet Cherriff, *Kurdistan und die Kurden*, Göttingen, 2 vols., 1986 and 1988.

Vanly, Ismet Cherriff, *Le Kurdistan irakien, entité nationale*, Neuchâtel, La Baconnière, 1970.

Vanly, Ismet Cherriff, *Survey of the National Question of Turkish Kurdistan with Historical Background*, Zurich, Hevra, 1971.

Weiker, Walter, *The Modernisation of Turkey: From Atatürk to the Present Day*, New York, Holmes Meier, 1981.

Weiker, Walter, *The Turkish Revolution, 1960-1961: Aspects of Military Politics*, Washington, The Brookings Institution, 1963.

Afterword

The situation of the Kurdish enclave protected by allied air power remains both precarious and paradoxical; in fact it depends on the survival of Saddam Hussein's regime.

The economic and financial position is poor. Restrictions due to the embargo, Turkish interference with the free passage of goods, and the fact that the UN continues to talk only with Baghdad all indicate that the *de facto* autonomy of Turkish Kurdistan is illusory. In practice, the Kurds of Iraq are living mainly off international aid.

Contraband and black market goods provide some economic leeway and prevent major shortages occurring, notably in energy requirements such as petrol, electricity and fuel oil. However Baghdad's withdrawals of the 25 Dinar note (and Tehran's circulation of forged bank notes) have greatly perturbed the fragile economic equilibrium of the region.

Three-quarters of the population are out of work in the urban areas where two thirds of the Kurdish population are concentrated. This is due both to Baghdad's policy of systematic destruction of the mountain villages, the traditional homes of the Kurds who have been relocated to strategic hamlets in the plain, and to the flood of refugees in 1991. About 2.5 million of the 3.5-4 million Kurds of the autonomous region now live in or around two towns, Erbil and Sulaymaniya. The region itself consists of a strip of land some 80-200 kilometres wide, and does not include either Kirkuk or Mosul, both still controlled by Baghdad.

What has happened since the election of the Assembly in May 1992 and its decision in October 1992 not to challenge the territorial integrity of Iraq, opting instead for a federalist solution?

Firstly, the 'Front' formed before the elections by the two main parties, Jalal Talabani's PUK and Masoud Barzani's KDP, along with half a dozen other small parties, remains essentially bi-polar.

Iraqi Kurdistan is led by two groups that compete with each other, cover the same areas of work and paralyse each other at the same time. The KDP is strong in Badinan and the PUK in Sulaymaniya. The 18 ministers have to manage a difficult situation and have set up an administration at *vilayet* (province) level under the authority of the *kaikmakam* (prefects). Power remains concentrated in the hands of Talabani and Barzani who both frequently travel abroad. All the evidence indicates that the roads are not safe at night. Whilst it is forbidden to bear arms in town, the same is not true in the countryside, where light weapons such as Kalashnikovs abound.

Secondly, after a year of tergiversation and peasant demonstrations, the assembly decided in spring 1993 to adopt a law on agrarian reform. Water and land problems are fundamental in the Kurdish areas (as in the rest of the Middle East). The three previous reform programmes (1985, 1970, 1979), all only partially put into practice, had left a great deal of land in the hands of the *aghas,* who were themselves very active during the 1991 insurrection. Putting the new reform into effect (land confiscation, redistribution or nationalisation) will take time and will cause many problems.

Thirdly there is the agreement with the Turkish authorities to eliminate the northern Iraqi bases of the PKK (the Turkey based Kurdish Workers Party). From early October 1992, Iraqi *peshmergas* clashed with PKK militants, who refused to abandon their bases near the Turkish frontier (Hakurk, Shivi, Haftanin, etc.). In mid-October, some 20,000 Turkish troops moved into northern Iraq on a mopping up operation. At the end of October, the PKK and the Iraqi Kurds signed an agreement stipulating that the former would no longer use Iraq as a logistics base.

Fourthly, the Kurds of Iraq formed an 'Iraqi Democratic Alliance' with representatives of the opposition to Saddam Hussein's regime. Unfortunately, this alliance, which sought to present itself as an alternative to Saddam, was not welcomed by Syria, which sees it as a US inspired initiative.

That broadly sums up the activities of the government over the last two years in Iraqi Kurdistan. Some mountain villages are being rebuilt, with the inadequate resources available. The towns continue to pose very serious problems, in that they are totally non-productive and expensive to administer. However the 1993 harvest was good.

Many highly qualified Kurds come to visit from America or Europe, but have to leave eventually as the government cannot afford to employ them. There is a shortage of political cadres and little effort is being made to train more, a characteristic of the Kurdish movements both in Iraq and in Iran. On the social level, the merchants are getting richer, the middle classes are under great pressure and much of the population is totally dependent on humanitarian aid. The government of the autonomous region finances itself almost entirely from tariff duties, amounting to some 90 million dinars, and estimates that 150 million would be needed for proper administration of the area.

On the military level, Iraqi Kurdistan remains very vulnerable. The armed forces are said to number 30,000 combatants, including about 12,000 from each of the two main political groups, equipped mainly with light weapons. In strategic terms, the capture of Zakho, on the Syrian—Iraqi—Turkish border, would make it possible to stifle any prolonged resistance.

In the short and medium term, the autonomous region faces two major internal problems. Firstly, it must lay the groundwork for an economy less dependent on international aid; secondly, it must create the basis from which a lasting military resistance could be maintained. In practice, the regional context appears broadly negative as far as the future of the Kurds of Iraq is concerned. In Iraq itself, Baghdad's armed forces number some 60 to 70 thousand well-equipped men, on the autonomous region's doorstep.

Iran, once on good terms with Masoud Barzani, is today mainly concerned with the systematic elimination of the KDPI. Following the assassination of Kurdish leaders (Vienna 1989, Berlin 1992), the Iranian airforce, in May and June 1993, repeatedly bombed positions held by the KDPI inside Iraq, close to the Iranian frontier. Since 1984, Iraqi Kurdish villages near the KDPI bases were also bombed, so as to turn the villagers against the organisation. Deprived of its best leaders (A.R. Ghassemlou's assassination was an irretrievable loss), the KDPI itself seems to be drifting without direction, at the mercy of events.

Syria, long the patron of Jalal Talabani's PUK, continues to back this movement, but never misses an opportunity to assert its authority and make apparent its displeasure at any Iraqi opposition or PUK contacts with the US government. Furthermore Syria has 800,000 to 1 million Kurds of its own, 250,000 of whom have no Syrian identity papers, and is fully aware that Syrian Kurdish volunteers are fighting alongside the Turkish PKK. Relations between Syria and Turkey remain strained (the problem of Alexandretta; the asylum granted to PKK leader 'Apo' Ocalan in Syria and Lebanon; Turkish pressure concerning the Tigris waters, etc.).

None of the states of the region approves of the idea of a territorial entity administered by the Kurds. Since November 1992, (in November 1992 at Ankara, in February 1993 at Damascus and in June 1993 at Tehran), Turkey, Iran and Syria, despite their many differences, have three times expressed their disapproval of 'the creation of a *de facto* Kurdish state' and their agreement concerning the need to maintain 'Iraq's territorial integrity'.

Leaving aside developments inside Iraq itself, Turkey is the most important state for the Iraqi Kurds. Following a long period during which the very existence of the Turkish Kurds was officially denied (1924—1991), Turkey, during the Gulf war, through its ex-president, Turgut Ozal, recognised the presence on its territory of some 12 million Kurds, representing 20 per cent of the country's total population. Some months later, Mr Demirel, the head of the Turkish government, referred to the 'Kurdish reality' in Turkey.

This recognition, granted *nolens volens*, was due above all to the operations conducted in Turkey by the PKK, which at the time was advocating secession. It also made it possible for Turkey to remind the world, in the middle of the Gulf war, that, should Iraq fall apart, Turkey might lay claim to the *vilayet* of Mosul, which Great Britain had joined to the *vilayets* of Baghdad and of Basra in 1920 and 1925 in order to form the Hashemite state of Iraq.

At the moment, Turkey constitutes and controls the only communication route between Iraqi Kurdistan and the rest of the world, a position that has enabled it to obtain the co-operation of the Iraqi Kurds in eliminating the PKK's logistics bases in northern Iraq. The PKK's offer to negotiate, in spring 1993, was not taken up. The PKK, the PUK and the KDP all feel that the death of Mr Turgut Ozal has frozen a situation that might have evolved into a promising dialogue. The current reality is that the Turkish Army is conducting a very energetic campaign of what is euphemistically referred to as 'pacification', deploying considerable forces, both of men and of equipment, in the process. The state of siege allows the isolation of Kurdistan and the elimination of all notables favourable to Kurdish nationalism. The villages where the PKK has established a clandestine political infrastructure are subject to systematic terror. The weakened PKK, operating amongst a population exhausted by the repression and under pressure to leave Kurdistan, is sorely pressed: the army seems to believe that a military solution is possible. The June 1993 wave of terrorist attacks on embassies and other buildings carried out by the PKK in Europe is its way of responding to the lack of international coverage of the war in Turkish Kurdistan, to which the Turkish government has committed 150,000 men. The August 1993 hostage-taking is part of the same policy.

Despite a relatively liberal facade maintained in eastern and central Anatolia, the reality is that since the recognition of their existence, the only thing the Kurds of Turkey have obtained has been the right to speak Kurdish amongst themselves in public. Turkey's position is further strengthened by the fact that allied air operations over Iraq are launched from the bases in Incirlik in southern Turkey.

Of the three countries who are concerned at the situation in the autonomous region of Iraqi Kurdistan, Turkey is the most determined not to allow a '*de facto* Kurdish state' to emerge in Iraq. After Israel and Egypt, Turkey is the third largest beneficiary of US aid in the region and remains a key ally for America. This gives Turkish policy makers considerable room for manoeuvre. Operations against the PKK will continue to seek to physically eliminate its support base, which leads the PKK to modify its strategy and turn to urban terrorism, with corresponding consequences for tourism in Turkey, an ever more important economic resource, especially since the dismemberment of Yugoslavia.

The main conclusions to be drawn from all this are firstly, the unanimous hostility of all the countries where a Kurdish minority exists to any change in the *status quo*, and secondly that the autonomy of Iraqi Kurdistan depends less on the efforts of the Kurds of Iraq than on circumstances largely beyond their control.

Index